Field Guide to
KNITTING

How to Identify, Select, and Work
Virtually Every Stitch

By Jackie Pawlowski

QUIRK BOOKS
PHILADELPHIA

DISCLAIMER: The knitting world is wide and varied. Although we have taken care to represent a large variety of stitches, the author and publisher cannot guarantee this guide addresses every possible stitch worldwide.

Library of Congress Cataloging in Publication Number: 2007929865

ISBN: 978-1-59474-158-6

Printed in Singapore
Typeset in Adobe Garamond, Franklin Gothic, and Impact

Designed by Karen Onorato
Iconography by Karen Onorato
Edited by Kevin Kosbab

Distributed in North America by Chronicle Books
680 Second Street
San Francisco, CA 94107

10 9 8 7 6 5 4 3 2 1

Quirk Books
215 Church Street
Philadelphia, PA 19106
www.quirkbooks.com

Contents

CABLES

OPENWORK AND LACE

RIBBINGS AND EDGINGS

Introduction

Stitch dictionaries can be sources of both inspiration and frustration. Flipping through large, glossy pages and gazing at lovely pictures of swatches can set your imagination in motion. But when it comes time to plan a project, real questions remain: How would this stitch work in a sweater? How much yarn will you need? And, perhaps most important, can you watch TV while knitting a particular stitch, or do you have to pay attention? Most stitch dictionaries leave you to figure out the answers for yourself—usually the hard way, after a sweater doesn't hold its shape, you run out of yarn, or the pattern is an endless challenge.

Field Guide to Knitting provides the inspiration without the frustration. In the pages that follow you will find the types of history and tips you'd learn by the side of a trusted friend and experienced knitter. This easy-to-carry book contains instructions for each stitch pattern along with such valuable information as the characteristics of the fabric it creates (Will it stretch? How will it drape? Does it lie flat? Will it distort?); the amount of yarn it will consume; the history and background of the stitch; and ideas for how each might be used. A small army of swatchers (made up of experienced hobby knitters, not professional experts) test-knitted each pattern to ensure clarity and to work through the sorts of questions any knitter might encounter. Color photographs of each swatch, great for pre-cast-on browsing, can be found in the glossy middle section. Be sure to keep this handy reference in your knitting bag, so you're always ready for trips to the yarn store or excursions to the fiber festival.

My suggestions for pattern use are just that—suggestions. They should motivate you to invent better ideas and uses. I hope this book will inspire fearless, adventurous knitting. Countless wonderful projects are out there, just waiting for a knitter like you to think them up.

Notes on Using This Book

YARN CONSUMPTION

The amount of yarn necessary to knit a given stitch pattern depends primarily on gauge, and as any knitter knows, gauge is a fickle creature, difficult to predict and prone to variations. The yarn consumption guidelines given in this book assume that the factors determining gauge—yarn type, needle size, tension, and so on—are constant. As much as possible, the sample swatches in the color plates were knit using the same type of yarn and the same size needles over roughly the same area of fabric.

However, this was not always possible. Some stitch patterns use a specific number of stitches within a repeat, which doesn't always measure up to the standard swatch size. Moreover, most lace patterns do not lend themselves to the same worsted-weight yarns used for the other patterns, so lace swatches have been knit using a lighter-weight silk-blend yarn. Such differences have been factored into the yarn consumption notes, and any exceptions specific to a stitch pattern have been noted.

In general, the text will use the following standard to indicate the amount of yarn consumed by a stitch pattern relative to standard stockinette stitch knit using the same needles and yarn over the same area. (Stockinette is also the benchmark for other characteristics, such as drape and elasticity.)

: These stitches patterns exemplify efficient yarn use, and they can generate vast swaths of fabric with a surprisingly small amount of yarn. Generally, these stitch patterns require significantly less yarn than it would take to knit standard stockinette using the same needles and yarn over the same area.

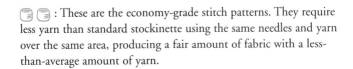 : These are the economy-grade stitch patterns. They require less yarn than standard stockinette using the same needles and yarn over the same area, producing a fair amount of fabric with a less-than-average amount of yarn.

: These stitch patterns require approximately the same amount of yarn as standard stockinette using the same needles and yarn over the same area.

: These are hungry stitch patterns. They require a noticeable amount of yarn beyond what is consumed for standard stockinette using the same needles and yarn over the same area. Plan accordingly.

: These stitch patterns are the black holes of knitting. Buy extra yarn when starting a project featuring one of these patterns, and then buy some more, just in case. Generally, these stitch patterns require substantially more yarn than it would take to knit standard stockinette using the same needles and yarn over the same area.

NEEDLE SIZES

The needle size chosen for a project is highly dependent on the type of fabric desired for the fabric and can vary widely. The needle size icon suggests the range of sizes to use to achieve a fabric with a clearly defined pattern when using an appropriate yarn weight. Pairing larger needles with finer yarn, or vice versa, may achieve different results—and that may not be a bad thing. Experimentation is highly encouraged.

Pattern Abbreviations

RH: Right hand.
LH: Left hand.
RS: Right side (front).
WS: Wrong side (back).
rep: Repeat.
*:   Marks the start of instructions to be repeated (when directed).

BASIC STITCHES

k: Knit. With working yarn in back, insert RH needle into first loop on LH needle from front to back, wrap working yarn around RH needle, draw back through front of loop to create new loop on RH needle, slip first loop on LH needle off needle, and let drop into fabric.

p: Purl. With working yarn in front, insert RH needle into first loop on LH needle from back to front, wrap working yarn around RH needle, draw back through front of loop to create new loop on RH needle, slip first loop on LH needle off needle and let drop into fabric.

sl: Slip stitch. Slip stitch from LH to RH needle without working it. Unless otherwise indicated by the pattern, slip the stitch as if to purl, without twisting its mount.

tbl: Through back loop. Work stitch as instructed (knit, purl, etc.) through the back loop to twist its mount.

yb: Yarn back. Bring working yarn to back of work.

yf: Yarn forward. Bring working yarn to front of work.

INCREASES

inc1:   Increase 1 stitch. Knit into stitch directly below first stitch on LH needle, then knit into first stitch on LH needle, and with both stitches on RH needle, drop old stitch from LH needle.

m1:   Make 1 stitch. With RH needle, pick up strand of yarn that lies between the stitch just knit and the first stitch on LH needle. Pick up this strand by inserting needle from front to back. Insert LH needle into strand from front to back and transfer from RH needle to LH needle. Knit into back loop of this new stitch.

kf/b: Knit front and back. Insert RH needle into front of stitch on LH needle and knit without dropping stitch from LH needle, insert RH needle into back of stitch on LH needle and knit, drop stitch from LH needle.

yo: Yarn-over. Use this increase only when a gaping hole in the fabric is desired. Bring working yarn to front of work, and bring up around RH needle to work next knit stitch.

kf/b/f: Knit front, back, and front. Insert RH needle into front of stitch on LH needle and knit without dropping stitch from LH

needle, insert RH needle into back of stitch on LH needle
and knit without dropping stitch from LH needle, insert RH
needle into front of stitch on LH needle again and knit, drop
stitch from LH needle. Two stitches increased.

yfrn: Yarn forward around needle. This creates a yarn-over between
a knit stitch and a purl stitch—it will also create a gaping hole
in the fabric. Bring working yarn to front of work, bring up
around RH needle and back to front of work, then purl the
next stitch.

DECREASES

Right Leaning

k2tog: Knit 2 together. With working yarn in back, insert RH needle
into both first and second loops on LH needle from front to
back, wrap working yarn around RH needle, draw back
through front of loop to create new loop on RH needle, and
drop both loops on LH needle off needle.

k3tog: Knit 3 stitches together. With working yarn in back, insert
RH needle into both first, second, and third loops on LH
needle from front to back, wrap working yarn around RH
needle, draw back through front of loop to create new loop
on RH needle, and drop the three loops on LH needle off
needle.

Left Leaning

skp: Slip, knit, pass. Slip first loop on LH needle to RH needle purlwise, knit 1, pass slipped stitch over the stitch just knitted.

ssk: Slip, slip, knit. Slip 1 stitch knitwise, slip next stitch knitwise, insert LH needle into the front of the two slipped stitches on RH needle and knit both stitches together.

sk2p: Slip1-k2tog-psso. Slip1 st knitwise from LH needle onto RH needle. Knit together. Pass slipped stitch over the knit together stitch. Two stitches decreased.

STARTING AND STOPPING

CO: Cast on using an appropriate method. The long-tail cast on is generally suitable for the patterns in this book unless otherwise noted.

Long-Tail Cast On: Make slipknot around needle, leaving yarn tail 4 times the desired width of cast-on edge. Take both strands in left hand and needle in right hand with short strand in front. Catch short strand with left thumb, so that the yarn wraps counterclockwise around the thumb. Lift long strand with index finger. Moving needle clockwise, catch strand going to index finger from under the strand around the thumb and draw through thumb loop. Let strand slip off thumb and tighten short strand and tighten long strand if necessary. Repeat until desired number of stitches are cast on.

Loop Cast On: Provisional cast-on method. Using waste yarn, make a slipknot around RH needle, leaving a short tail. Lift working yarn with left index finger, with your thumb moving away from you. Using needle, catch long strand of yarn after point where held by index finger and thumb. Draw into loop onto needle and tighten by dropping from left hand and pulling on working yarn. On next row (Row 1), work into cast-on stitches using the yarn intended for project. When ready to work from provisional cast-on edge, unravel cast-on waste yarn, pick up the free loops, and work in opposite direction.

Cable Cast On: Make a slipknot around LH needle. Using RH needles, knit into slipknot and place new stitch on LH needle. For next cast-on stitch, * insert RH needle between first and second stitch on LH needle and knit, placing new stitch on LH needle; rep from * until desired number of stitches is cast on.

Knitted Cast On: Make a slipknot around LH needle. Using RH needles, knit into slipknot and place new stitch on LH needle. For next cast-on stitch, * insert RH needle into first stitch on LH needle and knit, placing new stitch on LH needle; rep from * until desired number of stitches is cast on.

BO: Bind off. Knit 1 preparatory stitch. * Knit 1. On RH needle, slip second stitch from the tip of the needle over the stitch closest to the tip of the needle and off the RH needle; rep from *.

Knit and Purl Stitches

GARTER STITCH

General
Description:

Garter stitch derives its name from its earliest use in the
band at the top of a stocking—its horizontal ease made it
particularly suitable for stretching where stretch was needed
most. Despite modern-day knitters' preference for using
ribbing at the top of their socks, the name has stuck.

Properties:

Garter stitch produces a flat, reversible, even-tensioned
fabric that will not curl around its edges. Horizontal
purl ridges offset by knit troughs make it thicker than
stockinette, and its lateral spread will cause it to
appear more squat, as well.

Yarn
Consumption:

Alternating purl ridges and knit troughs pull in the
fabric, creating horizontal ribbing that increases yarn
consumption.

Suggested Uses:
00–12+

Its flat, reversible fabric makes garter stitch a favorite
for sweater edgings and baby blankets, though it is
also suitable for the main fabric of garments. For a
scarf with vertical stripes, use a long circular needle to
cast enough stitches onto a long circular needle to
cover the length of the scarf. Knit in garter stitch,
switching colors at whim until scarf is desired width.

Pattern: **ALL ROWS:** Knit.

2a–b. **STOCKINETTE STITCH**

Other Names: Stocking stitch.

General
Description:
Stockinette stitch is the grandfather of all stitch patterns and is what most people recognize as "knitting."
This basic stitch pattern dates back to the earliest
known knitted artifacts, such as a thirteenth-century
knitted sock from Egypt and fourteenth-century
European stockings. Though historians believe the
inherent elasticity lent the technique to garments
designed for the foot—hence its name and earliest
uses—stockinette stitch is versatile and used all over
the world for any and all types of projects.

Properties:

Stockinette stitch produces a flat, even fabric characterized by orderly rows of knitted Vs. Purly bumps
show on the wrong side. When knitting a project
intended to be flat, be wary of stockinette's tendency
to curl toward the wrong side of the fabric; a scarf
knit entirely in stockinette stitch can result in a long
tube and a heap of frustration. This curl can be
mitigated by knitting one inch (2.5 cm) of an even-
tensioned stitch pattern, such as moss or garter stitch,
along each edge.

Yarn
Consumption:

As the most commonly used stitch pattern, stockinette stitch is the benchmark against which this text measures yarn consumption.

Suggested Uses:

00–12+

Aside from socks, stockinette stitch is suited for any project requiring a plain, flat surface and a dose of elasticity, such as mittens, gloves, sweaters, hats, stuffed animals, cushions, cozies, or anything else a knitter might desire. Cell phone cozies, stuffed dinosaurs, and anatomically correct human organs have all been knit using stockinette stitch plus a few creative increases and decreases—the only limit is the knitter's imagination.

Pattern:

ROW 1: Knit.
ROW 2: Purl.

Variation:

Reverse Stockinette
In contrast to standard stockinette, right side is characterized by its purly bumps, the wrong side by flat Vs. Reverse stockinette is commonly used as the background stitch for cablework and in traditional Andean and Peruvian knitting.

ROW 1: Purl.
ROW 2: Knit.

3. 📷   **SEED STITCH**

Other Names: Irish moss stitch.

General
Description: The bumpy, textured fabric produced by this stitch pattern is similar to moss stitch and dot stitch, and as an added bonus, it is easier to read the pattern in the fabric than for either of those: Simply knit into each purl stitch and purl into each knit stitch as they appear on the needle, and there is no need to keep track of rows.

Properties: Seed stitch produces a uniformly textured, reversible, even-tensioned fabric. The small, diagonally stacked bumps for which the pattern is named can give the fabric either a delicate, graceful texture or a nubby, tweedy texture, depending on the yarn used.

Yarn
Consumption: Though the constant alternating between knit and purl stitches produces a slightly tighter fabric than stockinette, seed stitch does not use significantly more yarn.

Suggested Uses: The unobtrusive nature of the patterning makes seed
2–10+   stitch perfect for edgings or buttonhole bands and to fill background in garments—both over large areas and within traveling line or cable designs. It is not suited for variegated yarns or other colorwork, as the subtle patterning is lost in the color changes.

Pattern:

(multiple of 2 stitches + 1)

ROW 1: * K1, p1; rep from *, end k1.
ROW 2: * K1, p1; rep from *, end k1.

4.

MOSS STITCH

General
Description:

Seed stitch becomes moss stitch by doubling the rows
before breaking the rib pattern. Moss stitch produces
a slightly taller and more pronounced checkerboard
pattern compared to its little sibling, and its fabric
also appears more knitted than woven.

Properties:

Moss stitch produces a uniformly textured, reversible,
even-tensioned fabric, thicker than that of stockinette
and seed stitch. The broken ribbing gives the fabric
elasticity—though not so much as a true ribbing—
and creates shadows that suggest lichen clinging to
tree bark, allowing even a knitter of limited imagination
to see the origin of the stitch's name.

Yarn
Consumption:

Double rows of broken ribbing draw in the fabric,
increasing yarn consumption.

Suggested Uses:

2–10

Its consistent patterning makes moss stitch useful for
edgings, buttonhole bands, and to fill background in
garments. Its thicker texture also makes it ideal as the
overall fabric for a more structured cardigan or jacket—

it will not drape as loosely as stockinette. Like seed stitch, it is not suited for variegated yarns or other color-work, as the patterning is obscured by color changes.

Pattern: **(multiple of 2 stitches)**

ROWS 1 AND 2: * K1, p1; rep from *.
ROWS 3 AND 4: * P1, k1; rep from *.

5. 📷 **DOUBLE SEED STITCH**

Other Names: Double moss stitch, box stitch.

General Description: As the name suggests, this pattern doubles both the rows and columns of seed stitch to create a four-stitch box pattern rather than a single-stitch box pattern, resulting in a bumpy fabric with dips and protrusions vaguely reminiscent of bubble wrap. Despite this resemblance, it is an excellent substitute for stock-inette, giving a project an interesting texture while maintaining a consistent pattern and a somewhat comparable drape.

Properties: ↻↔ Double seed stitch produces a uniformly textured, reversible, even-tensioned fabric, looser than seed or moss stitch and with a greater lateral stretch, as well.

Yarn
Consumption: Double rows of broken ribbing draw in the fabric, increasing yarn consumption.

Suggested Uses: The even-tensioned reversibility and larger box pattern make double seed stitch a good choice for wide borders or large swaths of fabric in almost any garment, from a basic sweater to a fitted, knee-length skirt for a tweedy 1940s look. Like its relatives, double seed stitch is not suited for variegated yarns or other colorwork, as the patterning is lost in the color changes.

2–10

Pattern: **(multiple of 4 stitches)**

ROWS 1 AND 2: * K2, p2; rep from *.
ROWS 3 AND 4: * P2, k2; rep from *.

---

6. **RICE STITCH**

General
Description: Mini ladder stitch would be another appropriate name for this stitch pattern—its proper name refers to the individual purl stitches stacked vertically on a field of stockinette, but seen another way, those little grains of rice form rungs on a tiny ladder of knit stitches.

Properties: This pattern forms a spongy, stretchy, broken one-by-one rib. Although not reversible, the wrong side of this fabric is handsome in its own right—its texture is suggestive of a knitted plaid pattern.

Yarn Consumption: Although the ribbing is broken, it draws in the fabric enough to increase yarn consumption.

Suggested Uses: Rice stitch would be an appropriate alternative to almost any instance of one-by-one ribbing. Worked on larger needles with a lighter-weight yarn, the stitch creates a mesh pattern that has a little bit of depth— perfect for a simple and interesting openwork top to be worn over a camisole.

Pattern: **(multiple of 2 stitches)**

ROW 1: * K1, p1; rep from *.
ROW 2: Purl.

DOT STITCH

General Description: Another variation of stockinette, this stitch pattern breaks up a vast field of knit stitches with the occasional purl bumps that gives the stitch its name.

Properties: Despite its textured appearance, without enough purl stitches to make this pattern even-tensioned, dot stitch creates a fabric with characteristics similar to stockinette: medium drape, a dose of elasticity, and a slight tendency to curl around its edges.

Yarn
Consumption:

Without enough purl stitches to significantly draw in the fabric, this stitch pattern uses approximately the same amount of yarn as stockinette.

Suggested Uses:

0–8+

Dot stitch creates an interesting fabric for a sweater blouse or a handbag—its purly dots lend a hint of delicacy. For an added accent, try knitting the purl bumps with a second color. The standard pattern is given below, but experiment with the frequency of the purl stitches for interesting trims or other decorative fabric.

Pattern:

(multiple of 2 stitches)

ROWS 1 AND 3: Knit.
ROW 2: * K1, p1; rep from *.
ROW 4: * P1, k1; rep from *.

Variation:

Sand Stitch (multiple of 2 stitches)
The yang to dot stitch's yin, the wrong side of dot stitch appears rougher, with a deeper texture, and is often used for rugged sportswear.

ROWS 1 AND 3: Purl.
ROW 2: * P1, k1; rep from *.
ROW 4: * K1, p1; rep from *.

8a–d. 📷   **SIMPLE DIAMONDS**

Other Names: Simple brocade.

General
Description: This pattern of crisp, stacked diamonds with shared sides is formed by purl stitches on a field of stockinette and dates back to the seventeenth century. Its popular longevity is no doubt attributable to its simple, clean lines and has resulted in countless variations, some of which are presented below.

Properties: The lattice of purl stitches make this fabric less elastic than stockinette; the crisp brocade gives it a formal air.

Yarn
Consumption: Because the purl stitches are not arranged in a way that draws in the fabric, this pattern uses approximately the same amount of yarn as stockinette.

Suggested Uses: The diamond pattern would be attractive as a border—along the edge of a formal lace tablecloth, for example, should a knitter have the ambition for a project of such scope. For more immediate results, the pattern would work nicely in a sweater vest or a holiday stocking.
\ 00–12+

Pattern: **(multiple of 8 stitches + 1)**

ROW 1: K4, * P1, k7; rep from *, p1, k4.
ROW 2: P3, * k1, p1, k1, p5; rep from *, end last rep p3.

ROW 3: K2, * p1, k3; rep from *, end last rep k2.
ROW 4: P1, * k1, p5, k1, p1; rep from *.
ROW 5: * P1, k7; rep from *, p1.
ROW 6: Repeat Row 4.
ROW 7: Repeat Row 3.
ROW 8: Repeat Row 2.

Variations: *King Charles Brocade* (multiple of 12 stitches + 1)
This stitch has the unfortunate distinction of being
named for a pattern in the vest worn by King Charles I
of England on the day he was executed for treason in
1649. Despite the late king's disastrous rule, his fashion
sense has certainly stood the test of time.

ROW 1: K1, * p1, k9, p1, k1; rep from *.
ROW 2: K1, * p1, k1, p7, k1, p1, k1; rep from *.
ROW 3: K1, * p1, k1, p1, k5, (p1, k1) twice; rep from *.
ROW 4: P1, * (p1, k1) twice, p3, k1, p1, k1, p2; rep
   from *.
ROW 5: K1, * k2, (p1, k1) 3 times, p1, k3; rep from *.
ROW 6: P1, * p3, (k1, p1) twice, k1, p4; rep from *.
ROW 7: K1, * k4, p1, k1, p1, k5; rep from *.
ROW 8: Repeat Row 6.
ROW 9: Repeat Row 5.
ROW 10: Repeat Row 4.
ROW 11: Repeat Row 3.
ROW 12: Repeat Row 2.

Seed Stitch Diamonds (multiple of 8 stitches)
These filled, vertically stacked diamonds create an
embossed fabric suitable for an afghan square or as
an interesting substitute for stockinette in garments.
With a tiny bit of basic math, the diamonds can be
shifted or resized to suit any need.

ROW 1: K3, p1, k4.
ROW 2: P3, k1, p1, k1, p2.
ROW 3: (K1, p1) 3 times, k2.
ROW 4: (P1, k1) 4 times.
ROW 5: Repeat Row 3.
ROW 6: Repeat Row 2.
ROW 7: Repeat Row 1.
ROW 8: Purl.

Inverness Diamonds (panel of 17 stitches)
This fancy variation comes from the traditional
fisherman sweaters of this port in the Highlands of
Scotland connecting Loch Ness to the North Sea.

ROW 1: K1, p3, k9, p3, k1.
ROW 2: P2, k3, p7, k3, p2.
ROW 3: K3, p3, k5, p3, k3.
ROW 4: P4, k3, p3, k3, p4.
ROW 5: K5, p3, k1, p3, k5.
ROW 6: P6, k5, p6.
ROW 7: K7, p3, k7.
ROW 8: Repeat Row 6.

ROW 9: Repeat Row 5.
ROW 10: Repeat Row 4.
ROW 11: Repeat Row 3.
ROW 12: Repeat Row 2.

9a–c.

PLAIN CHECK STITCH

Other Names: Block stitch, dice pattern.

General
Description:
This simple checkerboard pattern is formed by regularly alternating blocks of knit and purl stitches. Similar to basketweave in appearance, differentiation is easy upon inspection: Check stitch forms contrasting boxes of equal size, whereas basketweave's purl bands overlap around shorter knit squares.

Properties:
The even distribution of knit and purl blocks make this fabric reversible, and the fabric's uneven tension gives the blocks a puckered appearance.

Yarn
Consumption:
The contrasting knit and purl blocks are not arranged in a manner that would cause this pattern to use significantly more yarn than stockinette.

Suggested Uses:
1–12+
The mock weave texture suggests a handbag with wooden handles or a baby bonnet with complementary ribbons. Check stitch would also be an appropriate stockinette substitute in almost any instance except a

checkerboard, as stockinette's flat fabric is better suited
to a playing surface.

Pattern: **(multiple of 10 stitches + 5)**

ROWS 1, 3, 5, 6, 8, AND 10: K5, * p5, k5; rep from *.
ROWS 2, 4, 7, AND 9: P5, * k5, p5; rep from *.

Variations: *Garter Stitch Check* (multiple of 10 stitches + 5)
Contrasting blocks resembling little flags are formed
by three bold garter stitch ridges and are crisply delin-
eated from their neighbors. The fabric is the thickest
of the three varieties included here.

ROWS 1, 3, 5, 7, 9, AND 11: Knit.
ROWS 2, 4, AND 6: K5, * p5, k5; rep from *.
ROWS 8, 10, AND 12: P5, * k5, p5; rep from *.

Seed Stitch Check (multiple of 10 stitches + 5)
If the garter stitch checks resemble little flags, then the
seed stitch checks are the racing variety, with little checks
themselves. These contrasting blocks are softer than the
other two variations and give the fabric a nubby texture.

ROWS 1, 3, AND 5 (WS): P5, * (k1, p1) twice, k1, p5;
    rep from *.
ROWS 2 AND 4: K5, * (k1, p1) twice, k6; rep from *.
ROWS 6, 8, AND 10: (P1, k1) twice, p1, * k5, (p1, k1)
    twice, p1; rep from *.

ROWS 7 AND 9: (P1, k1) twice, p1, * p5, (p1, k1) twice, p1; rep from *.

---

10.   **WOVEN STITCH**

General
Description:

Like stockinette, woven stitch is one of the most basic knitting patterns, forming a flat fabric with almost universal application. Its handsome woven texture is achieved by holding the yarn in front of the work—a technique beginners usually discover on their own, albeit unintentionally.

Properties:

The slipped stitches and horizontal stranding add subtle texture to a flat fabric; these elements also make it less elastic than stockinette.

Yarn
Consumption:

This pattern is essentially a variation of stockinette—as such, it uses the same amount of yarn.

Suggested Uses:

2–12+

Like dot stitch, the tiny lines interspersed among knitted Vs give the fabric a delicacy; it would work well for a sweater blouse or a summer tank. Working the stitch in two colors transforms it into a rugged and bold pattern, perfect for a tweedy fall sweater or a jaunty cap.

Pattern: **(even number of stitches)**

ROWS 1 AND 3 (WS): Purl.
ROW 2: K1, * sl 1 wyif, k1; rep from *, end k1.
ROW 4: K1, * k1, sl 1 wyif; rep from *, end k1.

---

11.   **RIBBED WOVEN STITCH**

General
Description: This clever variation of woven stitch makes use of
slipped stitches to create ribbing without having to
alternate between knit and purl stitches on the same row.

Properties: The ribbing creates a thicker, nonreversible fabric,
though the wrong side also has an interesting rib
design. At first glance, the patterning appears as a
stack of embedded boxes; upon closer inspection, a
tiny ladder design emerges, formed by the slipped
stitches between the knit columns.

Yarn
Consumption: This ribbed pattern draws in the fabric, using more
yarn than stockinette.

Suggested Uses: This boxy pattern would complement a boxy sweater,
2–12+   the sort that are often knit for babies, composed
entirely of rectangular pieces. Despite its ribbing, this
pattern will not cling to the shape of its wearer—
unless, of course, the garment is too small.

Pattern:

(odd number of stitches)

ROW 1: K1, * sl 1 wyif, k1; rep from *.
ROW 2: Purl.

12. **BASKETWEAVE**

General
Description:

This stitch belongs in the knitting pantheon alongside stockinette, garter, and woven stitch. Popular for centuries, it is simple yet clever looking, attractive without being ostentatious.

Properties:

Purl blocks overlap around knit blocks to great effect in this relatively flat fabric—their horizontal ridges emphasize the weave effect. The fabric is not reversible, as the purl blocks are larger than the knit blocks. This pattern uses five purl stitches in a block; others use seven, but in doing so, they run the risk of distortion.

Yarn
Consumption:

Because the knit and purl blocks are not aligned to draw in the fabric, this pattern uses approximately the same amount of yarn as stockinette.

Suggested Uses:
1–12+

A French market bag would be fabulous in this stitch, as would almost any jacket. All other factors being equal, basketweave won't drape as loosely as stockinette, making it a good candidate for any fabric requiring a bit more structure.

Pattern: **(multiple of 8 stitches + 5)**

ROW 1: Knit.
ROW 2: K5, * p3, k5; rep from *.
ROW 3: P5, * k3, p5; rep from *.
ROW 4: Repeat Row 2.
ROW 5: Knit.
ROW 6: K1, * p3, k5; rep from *, end last repeat k1.
ROW 7: P1, * k3, p5; rep from *, end last repeat p1.
ROW 8: Repeat Row 6.

13.   **RIBBED BASKETWEAVE**

Other Names: Double basket pattern.

General
Description: A variation of basketweave, this pattern also uses knit
and purl bands to create a woven effect. This is almost
the only similarity, as the fabric created in this ribbed
version differs drastically from its counterpart.

Properties: Perpendicular knit and purl ribbings create a
↔   thick, cushionlike fabric that will stretch in any
and all directions. Unblocked, the woven panels
will curl around their neighbors with gusto;
blocked, the ribbing will behave in a more orderly
manner. However, no amount of blocking, press-

ing, or cursing will force the knit ribs into crisp vertical lines.

Yarn
Consumption:

The thick ribbing draws in the fabric significantly, increasing yarn consumption substantially.

Suggested Uses:

00–12+

Pillows, cushions, the shell of a stuffed-animal tortoise, an extraordinarily baggy sweater—this stitch pattern will work well in any project for which sizing is not important. The perpendicular ribbings can cause the fabric to distort and stretch in odd ways, resulting in a garment with an unpredictable fit.

Pattern:

(multiple of 18 stitches + 10)

ROW 1: * K11, p2, k2, p2, k1; rep from *, end k10.
ROW 2: P1, k8, p1, * p1, (k2, p2) twice, k8, p1; rep from *.
ROW 3: * K1, p8, (k2, p2) twice, k1; rep from *, end k1, p8, k1.
ROW 4: P10, * p1, k2, p2, k2, p11; rep from *.
ROWS 5, 6, 7, AND 8: Repeats Rows 1, 2, 3, and 4.
ROW 9: Knit.
ROW 10: (P2, k2) twice, p2, * p10, (k2, p2) twice; rep from *.
ROW 11: * (K2, p2) twice, k2, p8; rep from *, end (k2, p2) twice, k2.
ROW 12: (P2, k2) twice, p2, * k8, (p2, k2) twice, p2; rep from *.

ROW 13: * (K2, p2) twice, k10; rep from *, (k2, p2)
twice, k2.

ROWS 14, 15, 16, AND 17: Repeat Rows 10, 11, 12,
and 13.

ROW 18: Purl.

14.   **SIMPLE CHEVRON**

Other Name: Zigzag stitch.

General
Description: A chevron is any V-shaped pattern, generally with its point
facing downward—though when connected lengthwise,
this distinction becomes irrelevant. This basic pattern
contrasts stockinette against reverse stockinette, but
the variations on the chevron theme are limitless.

Properties: The fabric formed by this pattern lies flat and is
reversible from back to front as well as from side to
side. The stockinette chevrons are raised from the
field of reverse stockinette, creating an illusion of thin
jagged strips outlining the thicker bands.

Yarn
Consumption: This pattern is even tensioned and uses approximately
the same amount of yarn as stockinette.

Suggested Uses: The chevron was popular in prints during the 1960s
00–12+   and 1970s; this patterning would be effective in a
retro tribute to the hip-length, flowing tunics of those

years. Its bold patterning also suggests upholstery and would work nicely for pillow or cushions.

Pattern: **(multiple of 8 stitches + 1)**

ROW 1: K1, * p7, k1; rep from *.
ROW 2: P1, * k7, p1; rep from *.
ROW 3: K2, * p5, k3; rep from *, end last repeat k2.
ROW 4: P2, * k5, p3; rep from *, end last repeat p2.
ROW 5: K3, * p3, k5; rep from *, end last repeat k3.
ROW 6: P3, * k3, p5; rep from *, end last repeat p3.
ROW 7: K4, * p1, k7; rep from *, end last repeat k4.
ROW 8: P4, * k1, p7; rep from *, end last repeat p4.
ROW 9: Repeat Row 2.
ROW 10: Repeat Row 1.
ROW 11: Repeat Row 4.
ROW 12: Repeat Row 3.
ROW 13: Repeat Row 6.
ROW 14: Repeat Row 5.
ROW 15: Repeat Row 8.
ROW 16: Repeat Row 7.

15.   **DEEP CHEVRON**

Other Name: Pinnacle chevron.

General
Description: An interesting illusion is created by the broken ribbings that form the sharp peaks and valleys of this pattern:

The fabric looks as though small cables were knit diagonally in a complicated fashion, but in fact it is constructed from a simple knit-purl combination.

Properties:
↔
The steep diagonal ribbing forms a thicker fabric with both a lateral stretch and a lesser vertical stretch.

Yarn
Consumption:
This pattern forms a deep, textured ribbing, increasing yarn consumption substantially.

Suggested Uses:
2–12+
With a little bit of shaping, the steep diagonal lines of this pattern could be cleverly used in a snug and curvy high-necked sweater. Its texture would also work nicely for a cushion.

Pattern: **(multiple of 18 stitches + 1)**

ROWS 1 AND 3: P1, * (k2, p2) twice, k1, (p2, k2) twice, p1; rep from *.

ROWS 2 AND 4: K1, * (p2, k2) twice, p1, (k2, p2) twice, k1; rep from *.

ROWS 5 AND 7: P1, * p1, k2, p2, k2, p3, (k2, p2) twice; rep from *.

ROWS 6 AND 8: K1, * k1, p2, k2, p2, k3, (p2, k2) twice; rep from *.

ROWS 9 AND 11: Repeat Rows 2 and 4.

ROWS 10 AND 12: Repeat Rows 1 and 3.

ROWS 13 AND 15: Repeat Rows 6 and 8.

ROWS 14 AND 16: Repeat Rows 5 and 7.

16.   **FANCY CHEVRON**

Other Name: Seeded chevron.

General
Description: An elaborate version of the basic chevron pattern,
seed stitch fills a purl border like lights on a marquee.

Properties: While not reversible, the wrong side of this fabric is
also attractive: The seed stitch nubs are not bordered
by a purl ridge; rather, the purl ridge forms a second,
complementary chevron line.

Yarn
Consumption: This textured pattern uses more yarn than stockinette
but not as much as deep ribbing.

Suggested Uses: While its texture makes this pattern ideal for upholstery, it would also be striking worked into a skirt
with a beaded fringe.

2–8

Pattern: **(multiple of 22 stitches + 1)**

ROW 1: K1, * p3, (k1, p1) twice, k1, p5, k1, (p1, k1)
twice, p3, k1; rep from *.
ROW 2: P1, * p1, k3, (p1, k1) twice, p1, k3, p1, (k1,
p1) twice, k3, p2; rep from *.
ROW 3: K1, * k2, p3, (k1, p1) 5 times, k1, p3, k3; rep
from *.
ROW 4: K1, * p3, k3, (p1, k1) 4 times, p1, k3, p3,
k1; rep from *.

ROW 5: P1, * p1, k3, p3, (k1, p1) 3 times, k1, p3, k3, p2; rep from *.

ROW 6: K1, * k2, p3, k3, (p1, k1) twice, p1, k3, p3, k3; rep from *.

ROW 7: K1, * p3, k3, p3, k1, p1, k1, p3, k3, p3, k1; rep from *.

ROW 8: K1, * (p1, k3, p3, k3) twice, p1, k1; rep from *.

ROW 9: K1, * p1, k1, p3, k3, p5, k3, p3, k1, p1, k1; rep from *.

ROW 10: K1, * p1, k1, p1, (k3, p3) twice, k3, (p1, k1) twice; rep from *.

ROW 11: K1, * (p1, k1) twice, p3, k3, p1, k3, p3, (k1, p1) twice, k1; rep from *.

ROW 12: K1, * (p1, k1) twice, p1, k3, p5, k3, (p1, k1) 3 times; rep from *.

ROW 13: P1, * (p1, k1) 3 times, p3, k3, p3, (k1, p1) twice, k1, p2; rep from *.

ROW 14: K1, * k2, (p1, k1) twice, (p1, k3) twice, (p1, k1) 3 times, k2; rep from *.

---

17. 📷   **WAVING FLAMES**

General
Description: Similar to pinnacle chevron, this pattern uses escalating broken ribbing to create embossed trapezoids that lean to the right, like flames whooshing in the wind.

Properties:
↔   The raised, textured fabric has slightly greater lateral stretch than stockinette. Although not reversible,

the wrong side forms an interesting twisting pattern known as seaweed. Block the fabric only slightly to encourage the pattern to pop from the surface.

Yarn Consumption:

Suggested Uses:

00–10

The broken ribbing does not draw in the fabric or increase yarn usage appreciably.

Suitable for any application requiring an interesting motif with mild ribbing, this pattern would work along the edge of a hat or on the cuff of a sweater. Also consider using it as an allover pattern in a sock for a chunky, textured look.

Pattern: **(multiple of 6 stitches)**

ROW 1: * P4, k2; rep from *.
ROW 2 AND ALL OTHER EVEN-NUMBERED ROWS: Knit all knit sts and purl all purl sts.
ROW 3: * P3, k3; rep from *.
ROW 5: * P2, k4; rep from *.
ROW 7: P1, * k4, p2; rep from *, end k4, p1.
ROW 9: P1, * k3, p3; rep from *, end k3, p2.
ROW 11: P1, * k2, p4; rep from *, end k2, p3.
ROW 12: See Row 2.

18. 📷 **PAVILION PATTERN**

General
Description:

Using broken ribbing to build a mock diagonal basketweave, this pattern of interlocking diagonals creates
an allover pattern reminiscent of parquet flooring.

Properties:
↔

The flat fabric has slightly increased lateral and horizontal stretch. The diagonal streaks of purl stitches
create an interesting pattern of shooting triangles on
the wrong side and give the fabric a greater tendency
to distort than stockinette.

Yarn
Consumption:

The broken ribbing does not draw in the fabric or
increase yarn usage appreciably.

Suggested Uses:
00–10

Consider this stitch as an allover pattern for sweaters,
jackets, or socks—its flat surface and diagonal lines
make it a lively substitute for stockinette.

Pattern:

(multiple of 18 stitches)

ROW 1: * K2, p1, k5, p7, k3; rep from *.
ROW 2 AND ALL OTHER EVEN-NUMBERED ROWS: Knit
   all knit sts and purl all purl sts.
ROW 3: * (K1, p1) twice, k5, p5, k4; rep from *.
ROW 5: * P1, k3, p1, k5, p3, k5; rep from *.
ROW 7: * K5, p1, k5, p7; rep from *.
ROW 9: * (P1, k5) twice, p5, k1; rep from *.
ROW 11: * K1, (p1, k5) twice, p3, k2; rep from *.

ROW 13: K2, * p1, k5; rep from *, end last repeat k3.

ROW 15: * K3, p1, k5, p1, k3, p1, k1, p1, k2; rep from *.

ROW 17: * K4, p1, k5, p1, k1, p1, k3, p1, k1; rep from *.

ROW 19: * K5, p7, k5, p1; rep from *.

ROW 21: * P1, k5, p5, k5, p1, k1; rep from *.

ROW 23: * K1, p1, k5, p3, k5, p1, k2; rep from *.

ROW 25: * K2, p7, k5, p1, k3; rep from *.

ROW 27: * K1, p1, k1, p5, k5, p1, k4; rep from *.

ROW 29: * P1, k3, p3, k5, p1, k5; rep from *.

ROW 31: * K5, p1; rep from *.

ROW 33: * K4, p1, k1, p1, k3, p1, k5, p1, k1; rep from *.

ROW 35: * (K3, p1) twice, k1, p1, k5, p1, k2; rep from *.

ROW 36: See Row 2.

19.

PENNANT STITCH

Other Name: Pennant pleating.

General Description: A geometric pattern of interlocking triangles, this Scottish pattern is named for its resemblance to vertically stacked flags strung on a line.

Properties: The neighboring knit and purl pennants draw in on each other, giving this reversible fabric a tendency to form pleats that are difficult to suppress even with rigorous blocking. Pleats aside, the fabric is not substantially thicker than stockinette worked with the same yarn and needles.

Yarn
Consumption:

The pleating draws in the fabric, increasing yarn consumption.

Suggested Uses:

2–8+

The pleating makes pennant stitch an obvious candidate for skirts. Worked on smaller needles, this pattern would also make an interesting edging on a modular sweater.

Pattern: **(multiple of 6 stitches)**

ROW 1: *K1, p5; rep from *.
ROW 2: *K4, p2; rep from *.
ROW 3: *K3, p3; rep from *.
ROW 4: *K2, p4; rep from *.
ROW 5: *K5, p1; rep from *.
ROW 6: Repeat Row 4.
ROW 7: Repeat Row 3.
ROW 8: Repeat Row 2.

20.   **PYRAMID PATTERN**

General
Description:

This Italian pattern uses knit stitches raised on a bed of reverse stockinette to form a series of stacked triangles.

Properties: The nonreversible raised pattern has an almost ruglike quality, and while it is named for its pyramid structures, the geometric triangles also resemble pine trees or arrowheads.

Yarn Consumption: The raised knit stitches create a mini-ribbing, drawing in the fabric and increasing yarn consumption.

2–8

Suggested Uses: Try this pattern on a winter hat, placing decreases within the reverse stockinette. The pyramid points will draw closer together as they approach the crown. The raised patterning also makes it suitable for a bedspread or an afghan square.

Pattern: **(multiple of 8 stitches + 1)**

ROWS 1 AND 3: * P1, k1; rep from *, end p1.
ROWS 2 AND 4: * K1, p1; rep from *, end k1.
ROWS 5 AND 7: * P2, (k1, p1) 3 times; rep from *, end p1.
ROWS 6 AND 8: * K2, (p1, k1) 3 times; rep from *, end k1.
ROWS 9 AND 11: * P3, k1, p1, k1, p2; rep from *, end p1.
ROWS 10 AND 12: * K3, p1, k1, p1, k2; rep from *, end k1.
ROWS 13 AND 15: * P4, k1, p3; rep from *, end p1.
ROWS 14 AND 16: * K4, p1, k3; rep from *, end k1.

21. 📷 **PARALLELOGRAMS**

Other Name: Vertical parallelogram check

General Description: While its name suggests a linear geometric pattern, the arrangement of the knit and purl blocks actually creates a curvy pattern—like interwoven ribbons or long hair gathered in bands.

Properties: The wrong side of the fabric is a mirror image of the right side. If using this pattern for a cardigan, or in any project with a center, reverse the pattern for the second panel to achieve symmetry.

Yarn Consumption: The offsetting knit and purl blocks do not draw in the fabric or increase yarn usage significantly.

Suggested Uses: Effectively reversible, this pattern would be great for a matching scarf and hat set. For something less ordinary, it would also add a nice woven texture to a shrug or a wrap.

2–8

Pattern: **(multiple of 5 stitches)**

ROW 1: * P1, k4; rep from *.
ROWS 2 AND 3: * P3, k2; rep from *.
ROW 4: Repeat Row 1.
ROW 5: * K1, p4; rep from *.
ROWS 6 AND 7: * K3, p2; rep from *.
ROW 8: Repeat Row 5.

22. 📷 **TUMBLING BLOCKS**

Other Name: Seed-stitch diamond brocade.

General
Description: This pattern has three-dimensional effects—tumbling blocks, oddly twisted stair steps, or even the sails of a windmill might be seen in its raised stitches.

Properties: This highly textured, reversible pattern creates a bulky fabric without much drape. The edges are similar to pennant stitch and have a tendency to pleat.

Yarn
Consumption: The knit-purl chevrons draw in the fabric, increasing yarn consumption noticeably.

Suggested Uses: Shaping this fabric is difficult without distorting its clearly defined images, a difficulty compounded by the fabric's structured stiffness. Modular garments, such as children's sweaters or boxy tops, are more suited to this pattern.

2–8

Pattern: **(multiple of 9 stitches)**

ROW 1: * K5, p4; rep from *.
ROW 2: * P1, k3, p4, k1; rep from *.
ROW 3: * (P1, k1) twice, k1, p3, k1; rep from *.
ROW 4: * K1, p1, k2, (p1, k1) twice, p1; rep from *.
ROW 5: * (K1, p1) twice, k1, (k1, p1) twice; rep from *.
ROW 6: * P1, k1, p1, (p1, k1) 3 times; rep from *.

ROW 7: * P1, k1, p3, k2, p1, k1; rep from *.
ROW 8: * K1, p3, k4, p1; rep from *.
ROW 9: * K1, p4, k4; rep from *.
ROW 10: * P5, k4; rep from *.
ROW 11: * P3, k1, p1, k4; rep from *.
ROW 12: * P2, (k1, p1) twice, k3; rep from *.
ROW 13: * P1, (p1, k1) 4 times; rep from *.
ROW 14: * P1, (k1, p1) 4 times; rep from *.
ROW 15: * K1, (k1, p1) 4 times; rep from *.
ROW 16: * K3, (p1, k1) twice, p2; rep from *.
ROW 17: * K3, p1, k1, p4; rep from *.
ROW 18: * K4, p5; rep from *.

23a–b. 📷

LADDER STITCH

General
Description:

This is a traditional pattern found on the sweaters worn by the fishermen of Guernsey and Jersey in the Channel Islands. These sweaters, known as ganseys, are different from Irish Aran sweaters because of their emphasis on knit-purl patterning; Arans are famous for their heavy allover cabling.

Properties:

As the name suggests, ladder stitch is a vertical, non-reversible pattern with knit stitches forming the ladder on a bed of reverse stockinette. Traditionally, this pattern was placed around the armholes of hard-wearing ganseys—its flexibility extended the life of the sweater.

Yarn
Consumption: The knit-purl ladder rungs draw in the fabric slightly,
increasing yarn consumption.

Suggested Uses: In current gansey design, it is often found flanking
2–8 cables on gansey panels. Outside the realm of fisherman sweaters, this stitch could be used for straps and
extended around the body of a knitted handbag,
emulating the stitched-on strap style popular for can-
vas and leather bags.

Pattern: **(panel of 16 stitches)**

ROW 1 (WS): P2, k12, p2.
ROW 2: K2, p12, k2.
ROW 3: P2, k2, p8, k2, p2.
ROW 4: K2, p2, k8, p2, k2.
Repeat Rows 1–4 until panel is desired length.

Variation: *Jacob's Ladder* or *Ladder of Life* (panel of 7 stitches)
This pattern is different from ladder stitch because it
forms the ladder pattern with purl stitches on a stockinette background.

ROWS 1, 3, AND 5 (WS): K1, p5, k1.
ROWS 2 AND 4: P1, k5, p1.
ROW 6: Purl.
Repeat Rows 1–6 until panel is desired length.

24a–c.   **LIGHTNING STITCH**

Other Name: Zigzag stitch.

General
Description: Many of the patterns found on early traditional
ganseys derived from the ordinary experiences of simple fishermen—ladders, waves, and trees are among
the most common patterns, along with the lightning
bolt depicted in this stitch.

Properties: The most basic version of a stitch with endless varia-
↔   tions, this lightning pattern is formed by a single line
of purl stitches running through a panel of stockinette.

Yarn
Consumption: The single line of purl stitches does not draw in the
fabric or increase yarn usage significantly.

Suggested Uses: In addition to its traditional place in the panels of
2–8   ganseys, this stitch could be used nicely as a simple
border along the button band of a cardigan or
short jacket.

Pattern: **(panel of 7 stitches)**

ROW 1: K6, p1.
ROW 2: P1, k1, p5.
ROW 3: K4, p1, k2.
ROW 4: P3, k1, p3.
ROW 5: K2, p1, k4.

ROW 6: P5, k1, p1.
ROW 7: P1, k6.
ROW 8: Repeat Row 6.
ROW 9: Repeat Row 5.
ROW 10: Repeat Row 4.
ROW 11: Repeat Row 3.
ROW 12: Repeat Row 2.
Repeat Rows 1–12 until panel is desired length.

Variations: *Heavier Lightning Stitch* (panel of 10 stitches)
This pattern has a wider band of purl stitches forming
a bold streak of lightning.

ROW 1: K6, p4.
ROW 2: P1, k4, p5.
ROW 3: K4, p4, k2.
ROW 4: P3, k4, p3.
ROW 5: K2, p4, k4.
ROW 6: P5, k4, p1.
ROW 7: P4, k6.
ROW 8: Repeat Row 6.
ROW 9: Repeat Row 5.
ROW 10: Repeat Row 4.
ROW 11: Repeat Row 3.
ROW 12: Repeat Row 2.
Repeat Rows 1–12 until panel is desired length.

Double Lightning or *Marriage Lines* (panel of 10 stitches)
The themes surrounding these double streaks are

intriguing—representing both the dangerous electricity of violent storms and the relationship between husband and wife.

ROW 1: K6, p1, k2, p1.
ROW 2: P1, k1, p2, k1, p5.
ROW 3: K4, p1, k2, p1, k2.
ROW 4: P3, k1, p2, k1, p3.
ROW 5: K2, p1, k2, p1, k4.
ROW 6: P5, k1, p2, k1, p1.
ROW 7: P1, k2, p1, k6.
ROW 8: Repeat Row 6.
ROW 9: Repeat Row 5.
ROW 10: Repeat Row 4.
ROW 11: Repeat Row 3.
ROW 12: Repeat Row 2.
Repeat Rows 1–12 until panel is desired length.

25. 📷   **HORIZONTAL ZIGZAG**

Other Name: Chevron stitch.

General   The chevron patterns found on traditional ganseys are
Description: usually simple versions of this universal theme. This
               horizontal border is often found separating chest panels
               from patterning on the body of the sweater.

Properties: This two-purl zigzag is not reversible and does not create any appreciable ribbing. It forms a sturdy, no-nonsense border, suitable for fishing sweaters.

Yarn Consumption: The narrow purl band does not draw in the fabric significantly; as a result, this pattern will use approximately the same amount of yarn as stockinette.

Suggested Uses: In addition to its traditional role as a gansey border, horizontal zigzag could be used as a band along an empire-waisted top or as trim on a hat or gloves.

Pattern: **(multiple of 8 stitches)**

ROW 1: * P7, k1; rep from *.
ROW 2: * K2, p5, k1; rep from *.
ROW 3: * P2, k3, p2, k1; rep from *.
ROW 4: * P2, k2, p1, k2, p1; rep from *.
ROW 5: * K2, p3, k3; rep from *.
ROW 6: * P4, k1, p3; rep from *.
ROW 7: * P3, k1, p4; rep from *.

26. **SLOPED LADDERS**

General Description: Another pattern originating from the ordinary experiences of fishermen's lives centuries ago, these simple diagonal lines represent ship ladders and are often found bordering gansey panels.

Properties: This single-purl diagonal pattern is not reversible and does not create any appreciable ribbing. The rungs are placed close together, and from a distance the pattern is not instantly recognizable as a ladder. For a more pronounced ladder effect, increase the number of knit stitches between the purl stitches and widen the purl band.

Yarn Consumption: The narrow purl bands do not draw in the fabric significantly; as a result, this pattern will use approximately the same amount of yarn as stockinette.

Suggested Uses: Sloped ladders aren't just for maritime wear—with the addition of a buckle, this pattern would stand alone as a scout-style cloth belt.

2–8

Pattern: **(multiple of 5 stitches)**

ROW 1: Purl.
ROW 2: * K1, p4; rep from *.
ROW 3: * K3, p1, k1; rep from *.
ROW 4: * P2, k1, p2; rep from *.
ROW 5: * K1, p1, k3; rep from *.
ROW 6: * P4, k1; rep from *.
ROW 7: Purl.

27a–d.

GANSEY MOTIFS

General
Description:
Stylized representations of everyday objects in a fisherman's life were often worked into the chest panels of ganseys. Unlike most stitch patterns, these motifs are not meant to be repeated—though they could be if two anchors or two trees add to the overall appearance of the project.

Properties:
These motifs incorporate twisted stitches, yarn-overs, and decreases to form their images. Generally, the fabric remains flat, and the patterns are not reversible—not an issue when worked into a sweater, but something to be considered before designing a sea-themed scarf.

Yarn
Consumption:
Over one repeat of the pattern, these motifs will use about the same amount of yarn as stockinette. Worked repeatedly over a large area, the marginally larger amounts of yarn these motifs use might be noticeable.

Suggested Uses:
2–8
Aside from traditional uses, these panels would work well individually as the tops of pincushions, or they could be worked together into a nautical-themed pillow for the beach house (or tiny city apartment).

Patterns:
Tree Motif **(panel of 21 stitches)**

The simplest of the motifs presented here, a stylized pine tree is formed using only knit and purl stitches,

similar to the technique used in the horizontal and
vertical gansey panels.

ROW 1: Purl.
ROW 2: K1, p7, k2, p1, k2, p7, k1.
ROW 3: P1, k6, p2, k3, p2, k6, p1.
ROW 4: K1, p5, k2, p5, k2, p5, k1.
ROW 5: P1, k4, p2, k2, p1, k1, p1, k2, p2, k4, p1.
ROW 6: K1, p3, k2, p2, k2, p1, k2, p2, k2, p3, k1.
ROW 7: P1, k3, p1, k2, p2, k3, p2, k2, p1, k3, p1.
ROW 8: K1, p5, k2, p5, k2, p5, k1.
ROW 9: P1, k4, p2, k2, p1, k1, p1, k2, p2, k4, p1.
ROW 10: K1, p4, k1, p2, k2, p1, k2, p2, k1, p4, k1.
ROWS 11 AND 12: Repeat Rows 3 and 4.
ROW 13: P1, k5, p1, k2, p1, k1, p1, k2, p1, k5, p1.
ROWS 14 AND 15: Repeat Rows 2 and 3.
ROW 16: K1, p6, k1, p5, k1, p6, k1.
ROW 17: P1, k8, p1, k1, p1, k8, p1.
ROW 18: K1, p7, k2, p1, k2, p7, k1.
ROW 19: P1, k7, p1, k3, p1, k7, p1.
ROW 20: K1, p19, k1.
ROW 21: P1, k8, p1, k1, p1, k8, p1.
ROW 22: K1, p8, k1, p1, k1, p8, k1.
ROW 23: Purl.

Flag Motif (panel of 19 stitches)

This seed stitch motif is based on the Bailiwick of
Guernsey's traditional flag. The twisted stitches in the

center create the inner cross specific to this island's emblem. Repeat Rows 2–3 before working Rows 4–6, and Rows 8–9 after Rows 4–6, to create a more balanced flag shape.

ROW 1: K7, p5, k7.
ROW 2: P7, k2, p1 tbl, k2, p7.
ROW 3: K7, p2, k1 tbl, p2, k7.
ROW 4: K9, p1 tbl, k9.
ROW 5: P2, k15 tbl, p2.
ROWS 6, 7, 8, AND 9: Repeat Rows 4, 3, 2, and 1.

Anchor Motif (panel of 15 stitches)

Some traditional Dutch fisherman sweaters feature a single anchor motif on the center of the chest; simple anchor designs are also used in panels on ganseys. This pattern uses twisted stitches to create texture and to differentiate the pattern from its stockinette background.

ROW 1: K7, p1, k7.
ROW 2: P6, k1, p1 tbl, k1, p6.
ROW 3: K5, (p1, k1 tbl) twice, p1, k5.
ROW 4: P4, (k1, p1 tbl) 3 times, k1, p4.
ROW 5: K3, (p1, k1 tbl) 4 times, p1, k3.
ROW 6: P2, (k1, p1 tbl, k1, p1) 3 times, p1.
ROW 7: P4, k2, k1 tbl, p1, k1 tbl, k2, p4.
ROW 8: K4, p2, k1, p1 tbl, k1, p2, k4.
ROW 9: K6, k1 tbl, p1, k1 tbl, k6.

ROW 10: Repeat Row 2.
ROW 11: Repeat Row 9.
ROW 12: Repeat Row 2.
ROW 13: K2, p11, k2.
ROW 14: P2, k11, p2.
ROW 15: K6, p1, k1 tbl, p1, k6.
ROW 16: P5, (k1, p1 tbl) twice, k1, p5.
ROW 17: Repeat Row 15.
ROW 18: P7, k1, p7.

Ship Motif (panel of 19 stitches)

While the tree motif on page 47 is simple in its technique, this ship motif is simple in its presentation. The lower, formed by coupled yarn-overs and decreases, represents the ship's body, while the upper represents the ship's sails. A variation of the ship motif is sometimes used instead of the anchor on the chest of traditional Dutch fisherman sweaters.

ROW 1: K7, k2tog, yo, k1, yo, ssk, k7.
ROW 2 AND ALL EVEN-NUMBERED ROWS: Purl.
ROW 3: K6, k2tog, yo, k3, yo, ssk, k6.
ROW 5: K5, (k2tog, yo) twice, k1, (yo, ssk) twice, k5.
ROW 7: K4, (k2tog, yo) twice, k3, (yo, ssk) twice, k4.
ROW 9: K3, (k2tog, yo) twice, k5, (yo, ssk) twice, k3.
ROW 11: K2, (k2tog, yo) twice, k7, (yo, ssk) twice, k2.
ROW 13: K1, (k2tog, yo) twice, k9, (yo, ssk) twice, k1.
ROW 15: K3, (yo, ssk) twice, k5, (k2tog, yo) twice, k3.

ROW 17: K4, (yo, ssk) twice, k3, (k2tog, yo) twice, k4.
ROW 19: K5, (yo, ssk) twice, k1, (k2tog, yo) twice, k5.
ROW 21: K6, yo, ssk, yo, s2kp, yo, k2tog, yo, k6.
ROW 23: K7, yo, ssk, yo, s2kp, yo, k2tog, yo, k7.

---

28. **BRIOCHE STITCH**

General
Description:
Of Eastern origin, brioche stitch is the basic version of a collection of stitches characterized by yarn-overs and slipped stitch combinations knit together on the return row. This technique generally produces a three-dimensional mesh, a common feature of fabrics produced by this family of stitch patterns.

Properties:
This stitch forms a soft, lightly textured fabric, and touching its spongy surface reveals its similarity to the well-known French bread of the same name. The reversible ribbings have considerable stretch: Two stitches wide at the base, they ascend diagonally to a single knit-stitch pinnacle, giving this fabric its distinctive appearance.

Yarn
Consumption:
The thick and fluffy ribbings increase yarn consumption substantially.

Suggested Uses:
00–10
Sturdily handsome on both sides, this stitch (knit in worsted-weight yarn) is a prime candidate for scarves—particularly for those who are fussy about

their neckwear. The deep, soft ribbings have an insu-
lating effect, giving brioche the added benefit of extra
warmth. Knit using a fine yarn and smaller needles,
the pattern will create a lace mesh with elastic qualities
suitable for long, fancy gloves or stockings.

Pattern: **(even number of stitches)**

NOTE: Slip all stitches with yarn in back. If used at bottom
   edge of the fabric, work the last row as follows: Omit
   the yo, (p1, k2tog) across. Be sure to bind off loosely.
ROW 1 (PREPARATION ROW): * Yo, sl 1, k1; rep from *.
ROW 2: * Yo, sl 1, k2tog (slip stitch and yo of previous row); rep from *.
Repeat Row 2 only.

29. 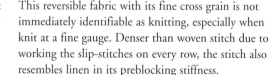 **LINEN STITCH**

General
Description:

This pattern uses slip stitches with the yarn held on the
right side to create a flat fabric with compact, inter-
twined patterning—its compact texture resembles its
namesake, the ancient textile woven from flax thread.

Properties:

This reversible fabric with its fine cross grain is not
immediately identifiable as knitting, especially when
knit at a fine gauge. Denser than woven stitch due to
working the slip-stitches on every row, the stitch also
resembles linen in its preblocking stiffness.

Yarn
Consumption:

Suggested Uses:

\ 2–8

A slip-stitch variation of stockinette, this pattern uses
approximately the same amount of yarn.

The stitch's inelasticity makes it more suitable for
carefully fitted garments or kitchen and bath linens.
With the wider availability of flax fibers, this pattern—
worked in linen yarn and edged with lace or other
woven patterns—would make decorative, durable,
and highly absorbent hand towels.

Pattern:

(even number of stitches)

ROW 1: * K1, sl 1 wyif; rep from *, k1.
ROW 2: * P1, sl 1 wyib; rep from *, p1.

30.

SLIP-STITCH HONEYCOMB

General
Description:

The honeycomb is a recurring theme in knitting
patterns, with numerous variations of lace, cable,
and slip-stitch patterns. It is named for its hexagonal
shape, similar to the wax cells built by bees to house
their honey. This version is not a true honeycomb
pattern, as its walls are not connected—rather, slip-
stitches of uneven size are stacked vertically, creating
an illusion of diagonal links.

Properties:

If it were named for its construction rather than its
appearance, this stitch might be called a garter woven

stitch. Its garter ridges give it a spongy texture, and while the fabric isn't reversible, its garter stitch basis gives the wrong side a honeycomb pattern similar to the right side.

Yarn
Consumption:

Because the spongy ridges draw in the fabric, this pattern uses more yarn than stockinette.

Suggested Uses:

2–12+

Worked on very large needles in a worsted weight or novelty yarn, this decorative and elastic mesh pattern would work nicely for a wrap. Worked in worsted weight with a medium-sized needle, this pattern would also be well suited for a shrug. Its mesh is attractive and its elasticity would provide flexibility for a garment that can be tricky to shape.

Pattern:

(odd number of stitches)

ROWS 1 AND 3: Knit.
ROW 2: K1, * sl 1 wyib, k1; rep from *.
ROW 4: K2, * sl 1 wyib, k1; rep from *, end k1.

31. SLIP-STITCH TRELLIS

Other Name:

Quilted lattice.

General
Description:

The names refer to the open cross-work pattern of slip-stitch laths stretching upward on a bed of stockinette. Another famous theme with endless variations, this basic version is efficient: The pattern is fairly simple, yet the fabric appears to have a complicated construction.

Properties: This nonreversible fabric would be flat except for the embossed trellis pattern criss-crossing its surface. Despite the raised patterning, the stockinette background gives it qualities similar to its base stitch.

Yarn Consumption: As a variation of stockinette, this pattern uses approximately the same amount of yarn.

Suggested Uses: While this quilted pattern would be attractive in a medium-weight sweater or a jacket, it would also be handsome worked into cushions for dining room chairs or to cover a wooden footstool. The modular patterning would make this a suitable pattern for variegated yarns, as well.

Pattern: **(multiple of 6 stitches + 3)**

ROWS 1 (WS) AND ALL OTHER ODD-NUMBERED ROWS: Purl.
ROW 2: K2, * sl 5 wyif, k1; rep from *, end k1.
ROW 4: K4, * insert needle under loose strand and knit next st, bringing st out under stand; k5; rep from *, end last repeat k4.
ROW 6: K1, sl 3 wyif, * k1, sl 5 wyif; rep from *, end

k1, sl 3 wyif, k1.

ROW 8: K1, * k next stitch under loose strand as in Row 4, k5; rep from *, end last repeat k1.

---

32. **WILDFLOWER KNOT**

General
Description:

Using a simple combination of yarn-overs and purling into stitches twice, this pattern creates a scattering of delicate wildflowers across a background of stockinette.

Properties:

The nonreversible fabric is slightly puckered around each flower, giving it the loose and carefree feel of summer. It is less elastic than stockinette; any application in which stretch is required could cause this fabric to distort around its designs.

Yarn
Consumption:

As a variation of stockinette, this pattern uses approximately the same amount of yarn.

Suggested Uses:

2–10

At first glance, the seemingly delicate pattern calls for dainty sweaters, summer blouses with ribbons running through eyelet edgings, and baby bonnets. But the stitch has a rugged side, as well—its wildflowers double as nubby cleats and would add traction to a stuffed toy ball. Worked on a tiny scale in white, this pattern could also be used to knit a golf ball.

Pattern: **(multiple of 8 stitches + 5)**

ROWS 1 AND 3 (WS): Purl.
ROW 2: Knit.
ROW 4: K5, * p3tog, leave on needle; yo, purl same 3 sts tog again, k5; rep from *.
ROWS 5, 6, AND 7: Repeat Rows 1, 2, and 3.
ROW 8: K1, * p3tog, leave on needle; yo, purl same 3 sts tog again, k5; rep from *, end last rep k1.

33a–b.

BRICKLAYER'S STITCH

General Description: This pattern creates bricks of purly bumps surrounded by mortar of knit stitches.

Properties: The pattern's uneven tension raises the bricks from their mortar for an interesting effect but also causes the fabric's top and bottom edges to curl up toward the right side.

Yarn Consumption: The alternating strips of stockinette and reverse stockinette create horizontal ribbing, increasing yarn consumption.

Suggested Uses: The pattern's horizontal ribbings would make a sweater tend to ride up toward the wearer's waist,
4–10h and the ribbing would cause any garment to be bulky. However, this pattern worked in cotton makes a dish-

cloth with extraordinary scrubbing abilities. It is particularly attractive worked in multiple colors.

Pattern: **(multiple of 6 stitches + 9)**

ROW 1: Knit.

ROW 2: Purl.

ROW 3: K4, sl 1 wyib, *k5, sl 1 wyib; rep from *, end k4.

ROW 4: K4, sl 1 wyif, * k5, sl 1 wyif; rep from *, end k4.

ROW 5: P4, sl 1 wyib, * p5, sl 1 wyib; rep from *, end p4.

ROW 6: Repeat Row 4.

ROWS 7 AND 8: Repeat Rows 1 and 2.

ROW 9: K1, sl 1 wyib, k3, *k2, sl 1 wyib, k3; rep from *, end k2, sl 1 wyib, k1.

ROW 10: K1, sl 1 wyif, k3, *k2, sl 1 wyif, k3; rep from *, end k2, sl 1 wyif, k1.

ROW 11: P1, sl 1 wyib, p3, *p2, sl 1 wyif, p3; rep from *, end p2, sl 1 wyib, p1.

ROW 12: Repeat Row 10.

Variation: *Bricks* (multiple of 4 stitches + 3)

This pattern creates a reverse effect of the bricklayer's stitch given above—stockinette bricks are surrounded by a purly mortar. The pattern is most effective worked in two colors, switching every two rows.

ROWS 1 AND 2 (FOR MORTAR): Knit.

ROW 3: K1, * sl 1 wyib, k3; rep from * to last 2 sts, sl 1 wyib, k1.

ROW 4: P1, * sl 1 wyif, p3; rep from * to last 2 sts,
   sl 1, p1.
ROWS 5 AND 6: Knit.
ROW 7: K3, * sl 1 wyib, k3; rep from *.
ROW 8: P3, * sl 1 wyif, p3; rep from *.

---

34. 📷   **BOW TIES**

Other Names: Little butterfly.

General
Description: This pattern uses slip-stitches to create a checkerboard
of pinched bow ties or butterflies, depending on the
viewer's perspective.

Properties: The flat, nonreversible fabric consists of a series of
slip-stitches on a field of stockinette. The long slip-
stitches give the fabric a delicate structure—it won't
hold up to hard wear or heavy use—and they will not
counter the fabric's tendency to curl along its edges.

Yarn
Consumption: The gathering of the slip-stitches increases yarn consumption.

Suggested Uses: A subtle pleating effect is created along the sides of
the butterfly wings, which could be put to good use
in a skirt. Also, with a beaded or ribboned top edge,
the fabric would make a unique clasp purse.

Pattern: **(multiple of 10 stitches + 7)**

ROWS 1, 3, AND 5: K1, * k5, sl 5 wyif; rep from *, end
       k6.

ROWS 2 AND 4: Purl.

ROW 6: P8, * insert RH needle from below under the
       3 loose strands on right side of work; yarn over
       needle and draw up a loop (gathering loop); purl
       next st and sl gathering loop over purled st; p9; rep
       from *, end last repeat p8.

ROWS 7, 9, AND 11: K1, * sl 5 wyif, k5; rep from *,
       end sl 5 wyif, k1.

ROWS 8 AND 10: Purl.

ROW 12: P3 * lift 3 loose strands with gathering loop,
       purl the next st and slip loop over purled st as in
       Row 6; p9; rep from *, end last repeat p3.

35a–b.   **MOCK CABLE**

General
Description:

This pattern uses the twisted-stitch technique, by
which the knitter crosses two or more stitches without using a cable needle. The one-by-one cross illus-
trated here is the most basic twisted stitch pattern,
and once worked, it is easy to see how the technique
can be applied to wider cables and other traveling stitch
patterns. This technique appears neatest when worked at
a fine gauge.

Properties: The ribbed fabric has two vertical rows of knit stitches
                 that cross every fourth row. These narrow cables are
                 essentially two-by-two ribs—although they are not
                 reversible, they will create a thicker fabric with a
                 shorter lateral spread than stockinette worked over
                 the same number of stitches.

Yarn   The ribbing draws in the fabric, increasing yarn con-
Consumption: sumption.

Suggested Uses: These cables will add interest to any number of projects.
                 For garments, consider it as an allover sweater pattern,
                 an accent to more complicated cabling, or decoration
                 on a pair of child's stockings. It would also be a hand-
                 some fabric for a shoulder bag or a cushion in a warm
                 and comfortable living room.

Patterns: ***Classic Mock Cable* (cables to the right; panel of 6
                 stitches)**

                 ROWS 1 AND 3 (WS): K2, p2, k2.
                 ROW 2: P2, k2, p2.
                 ROW 4: P2, skip 1 st and knit second st, leaving it on
                     needle; knit skipped st and sl both sts from needle
                     together; p2.

Tamerna Stitch (**mock cables to the left; panel of 6 stitches**)

ROWS 1 AND 3 (WS): K2, p2, k2.
ROW 2: P2, k2, p2.
ROW 4: P2, take right needle behind left needle, skip 1 st and knit the second st in back loop, then knit the skipped st in front loop, sl both sts from needle together; p2.

---

36.   **HERRINGBONE**

General Description:
If knitting were a science, herringbone would be a species of the genus chevron. The pattern is characterized by fine Vs with a delicacy reminiscent of its namesake. There are countless variations of the herringbone pattern, and this basic knit-purl version is worked using a simple method of increasing and decreasing in adjoining rows.

Properties:
This pattern was designed to resemble its woven counterpart, to good effect—by interweaving its rows, this pattern doesn't have the traditional appearance of a knit fabric. This is particularly true when knit at a fine gauge or with two colors.

Yarn Consumption:
The use of increases and decreases to form the herringbone Vs draws the fabric in on itself, increasing yarn consumption.

Suggested Uses:
2–10

This pattern is particularly attractive when worked with tweedy yarns or two colors. It has a tailored finish, making it a nice choice for a coat or a smart-looking pair of gloves.

Pattern:

(multiple of 7 stitches + 1)

ROWS 1 AND 3 (WS): Purl.
ROW 2: * K2tog, k2, increase in next st as follows— place point of RH needle behind LH needle, insert point of RH needle from the top down through the purled head of the st below next st, and knit; then knit the st above; k2; rep from *, end k1.
ROW 4: K1, * k2, increase in next st as described in Row 2, k2, k2tog; rep from *.

37a–c.

BOBBLE STITCH

General
Description:

Bobbles are raised bumps in the fabric formed using a combination of increases and short-row shaping, a technique in which the work is turned midrow and the most recently worked stitches are worked again. When creating bobbles, this technique is taken to the extreme: A few stitches are increased and worked multiple times more than their neighbors, causing the fabric to balloon outward like someone blowing a bubble.

Properties:	Bobbles are extremely versatile—they can be worked anywhere in the fabric, made any size, and arranged into any pattern. Three examples are presented below to illustrate the various possibilities.
Yarn Consumption:	Yarn consumption depends greatly upon the size of the bobbles, their frequency, and the background stitch upon which they are placed.
Suggested Uses:	Bobbles can add emphasis and texture to any pattern. They are frequently found within open cables, upon the ends of broken cables, along border edges, atop sharp corners, and on the faces of intarsia clowns. Although it may be tempting to insert bobbles everywhere, exercise discretion. Use the bobble wisely.
Patterns:	***Plain Bobble* (multiple of 6 stitches + 5)**

0–12+

These normal-sized bobbles are stacked diagonally on a bed of garter stitch. Experimenting with the number of increases or repeats will demonstrate the versatility of this technique.

ROWS 1–5: Knit.
ROW 6: K5 * (yo, k1) 3 times into the next st, forming 6 bobble sts; turn work and sl 1, p5 across these 6 sts; turn again and sl 1, k5; turn again and (p2tog) 3 times; turn again and sk2p, completing

bobble; k5; rep from *.

ROW 7: K5 * p1 tbl, k5; rep from *.

ROWS 8–11: Knit.

ROW 12: K8, * make bobble in next st as in Row 6, k5; rep from *, end last rep k3.

Variations: *Large Bobble* or *Bubble-Bobble* (multiple of 10 stitches + 2)
This pattern is from the region formerly known as Czechoslovakia and is a good example of the effect large bobbles can have on a fabric. The fabric resembles a foam egg-crate mattress (without the firm support). Knit and seamed into a circular ball, this would make an excellent stuffed toy for a pet.

ROWS 1 AND 3 (WS): Purl.

ROW 2: Knit.

ROW 4: K1, * (k5, turn, p5, turn) 3 times, k10; rep from *, end k1.

ROWS 5, 6, AND 7: Repeat Rows 1, 2, and 3.

ROW 8: K6, * (k5, turn, p5, turn) 3 times, k10; rep from *, end last repeat k6.

Blackberry Stitch (multiple of 20 stitches + 1)
A lovely example of the bobble put to artistic use, this pattern clusters bobbles into a triangular arrangement strongly resembling a berry. The vertical strips of knit stitches running behind the berries on a field of reverse stockinette add the hint of a stem or vine—they complete the pattern nicely. Try this pattern on

an afghan square or a small clutch, or add a single blackberry as an accent on a garment.

MB: (K1, yo, k1, yo, k1) into the same st, forming 5 bobble sts; turn, p5, turn, k5, then pass 4th, 3rd, 2nd and 1st sts separately over the last st knitted, completing bobble.

ROW 1: K1, * (p4, k1) twice, p4, MB, p4, k1; rep from *.

ROW 2: P1, * k4, p1 tbl (into bobble st); (k4, p1) 3 times; rep from *.

ROW 3: K1, * (p4, k1) twice, p3, MB, p1, MB, p3, k1; rep from *.

ROW 4: P1, * k3, p1 tbl, k1, p1 tbl, k3, p1, (k4, p1) twice; rep from *.

ROW 5: K1, * (p4, k1) twice, p2, MB, (p1, MB) twice, p2, k1; rep from *.

ROW 6: P1, * k2, p1 tbl, (k1, p1 tbl) twice, k2, p1, (k4, p1) twice; rep from *.

ROW 7: K1, * p4, MB, (p4, k1) 3 times; rep from *.

ROW 8: P1, * (k4, p1) twice, k4, p1 tbl, k4, p1; rep from *.

ROW 9: K1, * p3, MB, p1, MB, p3, k1, (p4, k1) twice; rep from *.

ROW 10: P1, * (k4, p1) twice, k3, p1 tbl, k1, p1-b, k3, p1; rep from *.

ROW 11: K1, * p2, MB, (p1, MB) twice, p2, k1 (p4, k1) twice; rep from *.

ROW 12: P1, * (k4, p1) twice, k2, (p1 tbl, k1) twice,
p1 tbl, k2, p1; rep from *.

38. POPCORN STITCH

General
Description:

"Mock bobble" is the closest label to which popcorn
stitch may aspire; although this stitch produces raised
circular bumps on a flat surface, strictly defined, bobbles are created by working back and forth on the
same row. Popcorn stitch instead creates bumps by
working stitches over the course of two rows.

Properties:

For simplicity, this pattern demonstrates popcorns on
a bed of garter stitch. It produces small, raised bumps
on a field of garter ridges. Generally, however, popcorns can be placed on a background of any stitch
pattern by increasing on one row and decreasing on
the subsequent row.

Yarn
Consumption:

The yarn consumption for popcorns depends
largely on the background stitch chosen as a plat-
form for their display. As given here, the pattern
will use more yarn than stockinette due to the
horizontal ribbing formed by the garter stitch
background.

Suggested Uses:
2–10

Popcorns could be placed throughout a fabric in infinite
ways—try ordered stacking or offsetting for an allover

beaded effect, or arrange them to form lettering or a simple image.

Pattern: **(multiple of 6 stitches + 5)**

ROWS 1–4: Knit.

ROW 5: K5, * (k1, p1, p1, p1) loosely into next st, k5; rep from *.

ROW 6: K5, * sl 3, k1, pass 3rd, 2nd, and 1st of sl-sts separately over the last knitted st; k5; rep from *.

ROWS 7–10: Knit.

ROW 11: K8, * (k1, p1, p1, p1) loosely into next st, k5; rep from *, end last rep k3.

ROW 12: K8, * sl 3, k1, pass 3rd, 2nd, and 1st of sl-sts separately over the last knitted st; k5; rep from *, end last rep k3.

Cables

SIMPLE CABLES

General
Description:

Cables are any stitch patterns in which multiple stitches cross over other stitches to create a twist in the fabric. Typically this is accomplished with the aid of a cable needle, a double-pointed needle that holds the first group of stitches out of the way so the knitter can work the second group and then return to the first group. These "simple" cables cross a number of stitches over an equal number of stitches, and each cross occurs at regular intervals, always in the same direction. Though cables are traditionally associated with fisherman sweaters—decorative cables also make garments warmer and more durable—they may be used for almost any application.

Properties:

Cables are commonly formed by crossing knit stitches on a bed of purl stitches, creating a thick, crossed ribbing. This ribbing draws in the fabric, giving it a narrower lateral spread than an equivalent number of stockinette stitches. Cabling creates a nonreversible fabric with odd puckers on the wrong side where the stitches are twisted.

Yarn
Consumption:

Suggested Uses:

2–12+

In addition to the ribbing, simple cables' twisting also draws in the fabric and increases yarn consumption.

Cables can be added to any project in which a thicker fabric and vertical patterning are desired. Cabled panels can also be placed next to each other to create an allover cabling pattern. For a simple cable project, try knitting 4x2 ribbed fingerless mitts and add cabling to one of the 4-stitch panels. Or try adding cabled panels down the front or the sleeves of a sweater. When two or more cables are paired around a central line, remember to use the left-cross (L) and right-cross (R) versions opposite each other for symmetry.

Generally, cables appear proportional when they are crossed at a row interval that is equal to the number of stitches in the cable—a six-stitch cable crossed every six rows, and so on. Use the tiny cable given here (also called four-stitch or 4x4 cable) to border larger, more complicated cables or to add a single cable accent along the side of a garment. The medium size, even proportions, and simple crossing of the regular cable (six-stitch or 6x6 cable) make it popular for basic sweater and scarf patterns. The large cable (eight-stitch or 8x10 cable) pattern, with crossings every ten rows, demonstrates the effect of a nonproportional crossing. The oversized cable (twelve-stitch or 12x12 cable) begins to stretch the limits of a single crossing; it is best suited for bulky sweaters, chunky bags, or any project requiring a large, rippled texture.

Patterns: **_Tiny Cable L_ (panel of 8 stitches)**

ROWS 1 AND 3 (WS): K2, p4, k2.
ROW 2: P2, k4, p2.
ROW 4: P2, sl 2 sts to cn and hold in front; k2, then k2 from cn, p2.

Tiny Cable R (panel of 8 stitches)

ROWS 1 AND 3 (WS): K2, p4, k2.
ROW 2: P2, k4, p2.
ROW 4: P2, sl 2 sts to cn and hold in back; k2, then k2 from cn, p2.

Regular Cable L (panel of 10 stitches)

ROWS 1 AND 3 (WS): K2, p6, k2.
ROW 2: P2, k6, p2.
ROW 4: P2, sl 3 sts to cn and hold in front; k3, then k3 from cn, p2.
ROW 5: Repeat Row 1.
ROW 6: Repeat Row 2.

Regular Cable R (panel of 10 stitches)

ROWS 1 AND 3 (WS): K2, p6, k2.
ROW 2: P2, k6, p2.
ROW 4: P2, sl 3 sts to cn and hold in back; k3, then k3 from cn, p2.

ROW 5: Repeat Row 1.
ROW 6: Repeat Row 2.

Large Cable L (panel of 12 stitches)

ROWS 1 AND 3 (WS): K2, p8, k2.
ROW 2: P2, k8, p2.
ROW 4: P2, sl 4 sts to cn and hold in front; k4, then k4 from cn, p2.
ROWS 5, 7, AND 9: Repeat Row 1.
ROWS 6, 8, AND 10: Repeat Row 2.

Large Cable R (panel of 12 stitches)

ROWS 1 AND 3 (WS): K2, p8, k2.
ROW 2: P2, k8, p2.
ROW 4: P2, sl 4 sts to cn and hold in back; k4, then k4 from cn, p2.
ROWS 5, 7, AND 9: Repeat Row 1.
ROWS 6, 8, AND 10: Repeat Row 2.

Oversized Cable L (panel of 16 stitches)

ROWS 1 AND 3 (WS): K2, p12, k2.
ROW 2: P2, k12, p2.
ROW 4: P2, sl 6 sts to cn and hold in front; k6, then k6 from cn, p2.
ROWS 5, 7, 9, AND 11: Repeat Row 1.
ROWS 6, 8, 10, AND 12: Repeat Row 2.

Oversized Cable R (panel of 16 stitches)

ROWS 1 AND 3 (WS): K2, p12, k2.

ROW 2: P2, k12, p2.

ROW 4: P2, sl 6 sts to cn and hold in back; k6, then k6 from cn, p2.

ROWS 5, 7, 9, AND 11: Repeat Row 1.

ROWS 6, 8, 10, AND 12: Repeat Row 2.

40a–d.

WAVE CABLE

Other Names: Ribbon stitch.

General Description: Popular in traditional fishing sweaters of the British Isles and the North Sea region, this pattern puts a small twist into the simple cable pattern to create a series of rhythmic swells.

Properties: These cables alternate the direction of each twist—first left, then right, or vice versa—so that the two waving ribbons lay upon each other instead of wrapping around each other as in the simple cable pattern. The vertical ribbing and twisted stitches create a thick, layered fabric, with a shorter lateral spread than stockinette.

Yarn Consumption: In addition to the ribbing, wave cables' twisting also draws in the fabric and increases yarn consumption considerably.

Suggested Uses: Symmetrical wave cables would nicely flank any
  \ 2–12+   rounded, balanced cable for a vertical panel in an
  Aran sweater. Though chain cable is the traditional
  favorite to partner with wave cables, also consider
  pairing wave cables with OXO or horseshoe
  (upward double) cables. With or without partners,
  wave cables would add decoration and substance to
  bulky winter boot socks or a ribbon effect to a
  shoulder bag.

Patterns: ***Wave Cable L* (panel of 10 stitches)**

ROW 1 (WS) AND ALL OTHER WRONG-SIDE ROWS: K2,
  p6, k2.
ROW 2: P2, sl 3 sts to cn and hold in front; k3, then
  k3 from cn, p2.
ROWS 4 AND 6: P2, k6, p2.
ROW 8: P2, sl 3 sts to cn and hold in back; k3, then
  k3 from cn, p2.
ROWS 10 AND 12: P2, k6, p2.

***Wave Cable R* (panel of 10 stitches)**

ROW 1 (WS) AND ALL OTHER WRONG-SIDE ROWS: K2,
  p6, k2.
ROW 2: P2, sl 3 sts to cn and hold in back; k3, then
  k3 from cn, p2.
ROWS 4 AND 6: P2, k6, p2.
ROW 8: P2, sl 3 sts to cn and hold in front; k3, then

k3 from cn, p2.

ROWS 10 AND 12: P2, k6, p2.

Variations: *Small Wave Cable*

This reduced version of the standard wave cable is more suitable for regular socks or other applications requiring less bulk.

Small Wave Cable L (panel of 8 stitches)

ROW 1 (WS) AND ALL OTHER WRONG-SIDE ROWS: K2, p4, k2.

ROW 2: P2, sl 2 sts to cn and hold in front; k2, then k2 from cn, p2.

ROW 4: P2, k4, p2.

ROW 6: P2, sl 2 sts to cn and hold in back; k2, then k2 from cn, p2.

ROW 8: P2, k4, p2.

Small Wave Cable R (panel of 8 stitches)

ROW 1 (WS) AND ALL OTHER WRONG-SIDE ROWS: K2, p4, k2.

ROW 2: P2, sl 2 sts to cn and hold in back; k2, then k2 from cn, p2.

ROW 4: P2, k4, p2.

ROW 6: P2, sl 2 sts to cn and hold in front; k2, then k2 from cn, p2.

ROW 8: P2, k4, p2.

41.   **CHAIN CABLE**

Other Names: Double ribbon stitch.

General
Description: Named for its stacked links, this pattern is essentially
two symmetrical wave cables worked immediately
next to each other. This pattern is also the foundation
for the Aran honeycomb, a famous fisherman-sweater
background pattern.

Properties: Symmetrical wave cables form an enclosed circular
ribbing with characteristics similar to the base pattern.
The highly embossed pattern is thick and creates a
chunky, nonreversible fabric.

Yarn
Consumption: Chain cable's thick, layered fabric increases yarn consumption significantly.

Suggested Uses: Traditional fisherman-sweater panels are a favorite use
2–12+   for this cable, but inserting a panel down the sides of
chunky, ribbed legwarmers would be a fun, modern
alternative. Also consider making a holiday wall runner
by knitting a single panel of chain cable in festive colors
and stitching bells into the middle of each circle.

Pattern: **(panel of 12 stitches)**

ROW 1 (WS) AND ALL OTHER WRONG-SIDE ROWS: K2,
p8, k2.

ROW 2: P2, sl 2 sts to cn and hold in back; k2, then
k2 from cn; sl 2 sts to cn and hold in front; k2,
then k2 from cn, p2.

ROW 4: P2, k8, p2.

ROW 6: P2, sl 2 sts to cn and hold in front; k2, then
k2 from cn; sl 2 sts to cn and hold in back; k2,
then k2 from cn, p2.

ROW 8: P2, k8, p2.

42a–d.   **SLIP-STITCH CABLE**

Other Name: Slipped cables.

General
Description: The twists in this pattern are created by slipping a
stitch for two rows, dropping it, and then knitting the
stitches out of order. The slip stitch is anchored two
rows previously and forms one long stitch that crosses
over three rows, rather than a cross of multiple stitches
over one row (as in the simple cable) or a twisting of
two stitches over one row (as in the mock cable).

Properties: A somewhat neater version of the mock cable, this
stitch pattern creates a flat, cabled fabric with a crisp
crossing. The yarn crossings around the slipped stitches
blend into the purl stitches on the wrong side of the
fabric, making it look similar to the wrong side of
simple cable patterns.

Yarn
Consumption:

This pattern creates a ribbed panel that draws in the
fabric, increasing yarn consumption noticeably.

Suggested Uses:

2–6

These cables would look nice as a detail in an intricately
cabled sweater knit in a worsted- or DK-weight yarn.
Since these delicate cables do not add significant bulk
to the fabric, they are nice as embellishments for the
band along an empire waist or as details added to the
back of knitted gloves.

Patterns:

Slip-Stitch Cable L (panel of 7 stitches)

ROW 1 (WS): K2, p3, k2.
ROW 2: P2, sl 1 wyib; k2, p2.
ROW 3: K2, p2, sl 1 wyif, k2.
ROW 4: P2, drop sl-st to front of work, k2, pick up
      dropped st and knit it, p2.

Slip-Stitch Cable R (panel of 7 stitches)

ROW 1 (WS): K2, p3, k2.
ROW 2: P2, k2, sl 1 wyib, p2.
ROW 3: K2, sl 1 wyif, p2, k2.
ROW 4: P2, sl 2 wyib, drop sl-st to front of work, sl
      the same 2 sts back to LH needle, pick up dropped
      st and knit it, k2, p2.

Variations:

Slip-Stitch Double Cable
This pattern works two slip-stitch cables side by side

to create a symmetrical panel resembling stacked leaves or small wineglasses, depending on whether they are worked downward or upward.

Slip-Stitch Cable: Downward or *Mock Horeshoes*
(panel of 10 stitches)

ROW 1 (WS): K2, p6, k2.

ROW 2: P2, k2, sl 2 wyib, k2, p2.

ROW 3: K2, sl 1 wyif, p4, sl 1 wyif, k2.

ROW 4: P2, sl 2 wyib, drop next stitch to front of work, sl the same 2 sts back to LH needle, pick up dropped st and knit it, k2, drop next stitch to front of work, k2, pick up dropped st and knit it, p2.

Slip-Stitch Cable: Upward or *Mock Gull Stitch*
(panel of 10 stitches)

ROW 1 (WS): K2, p6, k2.

ROW 2: P2, sl 1 wyib, k4, sl 1 wyib, p2.

ROW 3: K2, p2, sl 2 wyif, p2, k2.

ROW 4: P2, drop sl-st to front of work, k2, pick up dropped st and knit it, sl 2 wyib, drop sl-st to front of work, sl the same 2 sts back to LH needle, pick up dropped st and knit it, k2, p2.

43a–b.

DOUBLE CABLE

Other Names: Horseshoe (upward), fishtail (downward).

General
Description:

In a double cable pattern, two symmetrical cables are worked side by side to create a balanced cable panel. In this case, two simple cables are paired to make a popular Aran pattern.

Properties:

Look closely to see that, in addition to being made up of horseshoes and fishtails, this pattern is an interwoven chain cable. It also has characteristics similar to chain cable—a highly embossed, layered fabric with bulky ribbing.

Yarn
Consumption:

The double crossings and thick ribbing increase yarn consumption significantly.

Suggested Uses:

2–12+

Popular as a panel down the center of a V-neck sweater, this pattern would add textural interest to any thick winter sweater. It would also make an excellent border on a lap blanket.

Patterns:

Double Cable: Horseshoe (panel of 12 stitches)

ROW 1 (WS) AND ALL OTHER WRONG-SIDE ROWS: K2, p8, k2
ROW 2: P2, sl 2 sts to cn and hold in back; k2, then k2 from cn, sl 2 sts to cn and hold in front; k2, then k2 from cn, p2.
ROWS 4, 6, AND 8: P2, k8, p2.

Reverse Double Cable: Fishtail (panel of 12 stitches)

ROW 1 (WS) AND ALL OTHER WRONG-SIDE ROWS: K2, p8, k2

ROW 2: P2, sl 2 sts to cn and hold in front; k2, then k2 from cn, sl 2 sts to cn and hold in back; k2, then k2 from cn, p2.

ROWS 4, 6, AND 8: P2, k8, p2.

44. **OXO CABLE**

Other Name: Noughts and crosses.

General Description:
This clever pattern is essentially a chain cable with a case of the hiccups. Its interrupted staggering creates alternating Xs and Os stacked in a vertical panel.

Properties:
The staggered design of this pattern creates an embossed panel with a relatively straight vertical edge—unlike most cable panels, which have curvy outlines. The dense, embossed fabric has deeply ribbed edges.

Yarn Consumption:
The deep ribbing and dense cabling increase yarn consumption noticeably.

2–12+

Suggested Uses:
The compact patterning makes OXO cables unsuitable for an allover pattern unless a dense, thickly textured

fabric is desirable for the project, as in the case of a winter scarf. Try knitting three panels side by side, with or without a plain rib as separation, for a warm and thick neck wrap. Consider starting the second panel on row 8 to offset the patterning.

Pattern: **(panel of 12 stitches)**

ROWS 1 AND 3 (WS): K2, p8, k2.

ROW 2: P2, k8, p2.

ROW 4: P2, sl 2 sts to cn and hold in back; k2, then k2 from cn; sl 2 sts to cn and hold in front; k2, then k2 from cn, p2.

ROWS 5, 6, AND 7: Repeat Rows 1, 2, and 3.

ROW 8: P2, sl2 sts to cn and hold in front; k2, then k2 from cn; sl 2 sts to cn and hold in back; k2, then k2 from cn, p2.

ROWS 9–12: Repeat Rows 5–8.

ROWS 13–16: Repeat Rows 1–4.

45a–b.

HONEYCOMB

General Description:

This allover pattern is famous for its use as a broad panel in sweaters in the Aran tradition. In popular belief, this patterning was used on fishing ganseys to represent the hardworking bee, but this myth likely developed with the budding commercial gansey industry in the early 1900s.

Properties:	Offsetting wave cables worked side by side creates a thick pattern of diagonally stacked, indented circles against a background of raised, curving stockinette. The fabric has little propensity to drape unless worked on needles a few sizes too big for the yarn, which would diminish the pattern's effect.
Yarn Consumption:	The layered cabling draws in the fabric, increasing yarn consumption substantially.
Suggested Uses: 2–12+	Along with its popular use as a broad panel down the front of a sweater, this pattern makes for warm and thickly cushioned boot socks.
Pattern:	**(multiple of 8 stitches + 2)**

ROW 1: Knit.

ROW 2 AND ALL OTHER EVEN-NUMBERED ROWS: Purl.

ROW 3: K1, * sl 2 sts to cn and hold in back; k2, then k2 from cn; sl 2 sts to cn and hold in front; k2, then k2 from cn; rep from *, k1.

ROW 5: Knit.

ROW 7: K1, * sl 2 sts to cn and hold in front; k2, then k2 from cn; sl 2 sts to cn and hold in back; k2, then k2 from cn; rep from *, k1.

Variation: *Tiny Honeycomb* (multiple of 6 stitches + 2)
Try this smaller version of the honeycomb for less bulky socks or for a simple, textured hat.

ROW 1: Knit.

ROW 2 AND ALL OTHER EVEN-NUMBERED ROWS: Purl.

ROW 3: K1, * sl 1 st to cn and hold in back; k2, then
k1 from cn; sl next 2 sts to cn and hold in front; k1,
then k2 from cn; rep from *, k1.

ROW 5: Knit.

ROW 7: K1, * sl 2 sts to cn and hold in front; k1,
then k2 from cn; sl next st to cn and hold in back;
k2, then k1 from cn; rep from *, k1.

ROW 8: See Row 2.

46a–d.

STAGHORN CABLE

General
Description:
Simple, U-shaped curves, slightly more defined than
for other cables of this variety, give this cable its name—
a slight misnomer, as deer have antlers, not horns.

Properties:
This wide cable is formed by diagonal strips of stockinette traveling away from a center cord. It creates a
thick fabric with elements of both vertical and horizontal ribbing.

Yarn
Consumption:
The layered cabling draws in the fabric, increasing
yarn consumption substantially.

Suggested Uses:
2–12+
A flatter, wider alternative to the double cable, this
symmetrical pattern is also suited for the center cable
in an Aran composition. Try knitting it up to the tip

of a V-neck and then splitting off the two last cable
cords to work as simple cables along the neck edge.

Pattern: **(panel of 20 stitches)**

BC: Sl 2 sts to cn and hold in back, k2, then k2 from cn.
FC: Sl 2 sts to cn and hold in front, k2, then k2 from cn.

ROW 1 (WS) AND ALL OTHER WRONG-SIDE ROWS: K2,
    p16, k2.
ROW 2: P2, k4, BC, FC, k4, p2.
ROW 4: P2, k2, BC, k4, FC, k2, p2.
ROW 6: P2, BC, k8, FC, p2.

Variations: *Reverse Staghorn Cable* (panel of 20 stitches)
This creates an upside-down V-shaped cable. It can be
worked immediately next to the staghorn cable, overlapping the end/beginning k2, to create a deep, cabled
chevron pattern.

ROW 1 (WS) AND ALL OTHER WRONG-SIDE ROWS: K2,
    p16, k2.
ROW 2: P2, FC, k8, BC, p2.
ROW 4: P2, k2, FC, k4, BC, k2, p2.
ROW 6: P2, k4, FC, BC, k4, p2.

Small Staghorn Cable (panel of 11 stitches)
Try one of these delicate, fluttering cables—formed
with the same method—down each side of a DK-weight

summer blouse for a mock ruffle.

ROW 1 (WS) AND ALL OTHER WRONG-SIDE ROWS: K2,
  p7, k2.
ROW 2: P2, k7, p2.
ROW 4: P2, sl 2 sts to cn and hold in back; k1, then
  k2 from cn, k1, sl 1 st to cn and hold in front; k2,
  then k1 from cn, p2.

Reverse Small Staghorn Cable (panel of 11 stitches)
This upside-down version of the small staghorn cable
has a similar mock-ruffle feel that would nicely accent
a dot-stitch or wildflower patterned handbag.

ROW 1 (WS) AND ALL OTHER WRONG-SIDE ROWS: K2,
  p7, k2.
ROW 2: P2, k7, p2.
ROW 4: P2, sl 1 st to cn and hold in front; k2, then
  k1 from cn, k1, sl 2 sts to cn and hold in back; k1,
  then k2 from cn, p2.

SMALL SYNCOPATED CABLE

Other Name: Twin waves.

General   Though this name could apply to any cable in which
Description: the traveling bands are not evenly offset, this cable is
              a good example of the concept. An offshoot of the

ribbon-stitch theme, the front wave is made up of
two twisting cables, giving it two crests. Neither crest
peaks opposite the back wave's crest.

Properties: The pattern's three stockinette cords intertwine
against a background of reverse stockinette to create a
thick, unevenly layered fabric.

Yarn
Consumption: The layered cabling draws in the fabric, increasing
yarn consumption substantially.

Suggested Uses: The relatively slim width makes this pattern a good
2–12+ choice for an intricate vertical panel to flank a wider,
openwork cable panel down the front of an Aran-style
sweater. The patterning is also reminiscent of wavy
locks and would be interesting worked onto the head
of a doll in hair-colored yarn.

Patterns: **BC:** Sl 2 sts to cn and hold in back, k2, then p2 from cn.
BKC: Sl 2 sts to cn and hold in back, k2, then k2
from cn.
FC: Sl 2 sts to cn and hold in front, p2, then k2 from cn.
FKC: Sl 2 sts to cn and hold in front, k2, then k2
from cn.
SBC: Sl 1 st to cn and hold in back, k2, then p1 from cn.
SFC: Sl 2 sts to cn and hold in front, p1, then k2
from cn.

(panel of 15 stitches)

ROWS 1 AND 3 (WS): K3, p4, k4, p2, k2.
ROW 2: P2, k2, p4, BKC, p3.
ROW 4: P2, FC, BC, k2, p3.
ROW 5 AND ALL SUBSEQUENT WRONG-SIDE ROWS:
   Knit all knit sts and purl all purl sts.
ROW 6: P4, BC, p1, SBC, p3.
ROW 8: P3, SBC, p1, BKC, p4.
ROW 10: P3, k2, BC, FC, p2.
ROW 12: P3, BKC, p4, k2, p2.
ROW 14: P3, k2, FC, BC, p2.
ROW 16: P3, SFC, p1, FC, p4.
ROW 18: P4, FKC, p1, SFC, p3.
ROW 20: P2, BC, FC, k2, p3.

Reverse Small Syncopated Cable **(panel of 15 stitches)**

ROW 1 (WS): (K2, p2) 3 times, k3.
ROW 2: P3, BKC, p4, k2, p2.
ROW 3 AND ALL SUBSEQUENT WRONG-SIDE ROWS:
   Knit all knit sts and purl all purl sts.
ROW 4: P3, k2, FC, BC, p2.
ROW 6: P3, SFC, p1, FC, p4.
ROW 8: P4, FKC, p1, SFC, p3.
ROW 10: P2, BC, FC, k2, p3.
ROW 12: P2, k2, p4, BKC, p3.
ROW 14: P2, FC, BC, k2, p3.
ROW 16: P4, BC, p1, SBC, p3.

ROW 18: P3, SBC, p1, BKC, p4.
ROW 20: P3, k2, BC, FC, p2.

48a–b.

OPEN SYNCOPATED CABLE

Other Name: Double-wrapped braid.

General Description: This open cable pattern has elements of the wave cable and the double helix, with a double wrap to add a hitch to the syncopation.

Properties: The pattern is worked by creating traveling stockinette bands over a bed of reverse stockinette; however, the bands have greater swaths of background between them than the small syncopated cable, creating a fabric that is not as dense, with a slightly looser drape. The long traveling bands have a tendency to wobble— even tension and careful blocking should help keep them straight.

Yarn Consumption: The layered cabling draws in the fabric, but the effect is offset by the open spaces between cables, causing the pattern to increase yarn consumption noticeably but not substantially.

Suggested Uses: The wide, open patterning and unconventional twisting would make symmetrical panels of this cable an interesting addition down the front of a tunic.

2–12+

Inserted into a bed of stockinette, it would indent nicely into the fabric.

Patterns:

(panel of 22 stitches)

BC: Sl 2 sts to cn and hold in back, k2, then p2 from cn.
BKC: Sl 2 sts to cn and hold in back, k2, then k2 from cn.
FC: Sl 2 sts to cn and hold in front, p2, then k2 from cn.
FKC: Sl 2 sts to cn and hold in front, k2, then k2 from cn.
SBC: Sl 1 st to cn and hold in back, k2, then p1 from cn.
SFC: Sl 2 sts to cn and hold in front, p1, then k2 from cn.

ROWS 1 AND 3 (WS): K5, p4, k8, p2, k3.
ROW 2: P3, k2, p8, k4, p5.
ROW 4: P3, FC, p6, FKC, p5.
ROW 5 AND ALL SUBSEQUENT WRONG-SIDE ROWS:
    Knit all knit sts and purl all purl sts.
ROW 6: P5, FC, p2, BC, FC, p3.
ROW 8: P7, k2, BC, p4, k2, p3.
ROW 10: P7, BKC, p4, BC, p3.
ROW 12: P5, BC, FC, BC, p5.
ROW 14: P3, BC, p4, FKC, p7.
ROW 16: P3, k2, p4, BC, k2, p7.
ROW 18: P3, FC, BC, p2, FC, p5.
ROW 20: P5, BKC, p6, FC, p3.
ROW 22: P5, k4, p8, k2, p3.

ROW 24: P5, BKC, p6, BC, p3.
ROW 26: P3, BC, FC, p2, BC, p5.
ROW 28: P3, k2, p4, FC, k2, p7.
ROW 30: P3, FC, p4, FKC, p7.
ROW 32: P5, FC, BC, FC, p5.
ROW 34: P7, BKC, p4, FC, p3.
ROW 36: P7, k2, FC, p4, k2, p3.
ROW 38: P5, BC, p2, FC, BC, p3.
ROW 40: P3, BC, p6, FKC, p5.

Reverse Open Syncopated Cable (panel of 22 stitches)

ROW 1 (WS): K5, p4, k8, p2, k3
ROW 2: P5, k4, p8, k2, p3.
ROW 3 AND ALL SUBSEQUENT WRONG-SIDE ROWS:
   Knit all knit sts, purl all purl sts.
ROW 4: P5, BKC, p6, BC, p3.
ROW 6: P3, BC, FC, p2, BC, p5.
ROW 8: P3, k2, p4, FC, k2, p7.
ROW 10: P3, FC, p4, FKC, p7.
ROW 12: P5, FC, BC, FC, p5.
ROW 14: P7, BKC, p4, FC, p3.
ROW 16: P7, k2, FC, p4, k2, p3.
ROW 18: P5, BC, p2, FC, BC, p3.
ROW 20: P3, BC, p6, FKC, p5.
ROW 22: P3, k2, p8, k4, p5.
ROW 24: P3, FC, p6, FKC, p5.
ROW 26: P5, FC, p2, BC, FC, p3.
ROW 28: P7, k2, BC, p4, k2, p3.

ROW 30: P7, BKC, p4, BC, p3.
ROW 32: P5, BC, FC, BC, p5.
ROW 34: P3, BC, p4, FKC, p7.
ROW 36: P3, k2, p4, BC, k2, p7.
ROW 38: P3, FC, BC, p2, FC, p5.
ROW 40: P5, BKC, p6, FC, p3.

49a–b.

TREE CABLE

Other Names: Reverse cupped cable.

General
Description: This is a simple broken-cable pattern: Two small bands of traveling stitches cross in the center and move down and outward to emulate the branches on a pine tree.

Properties: Because the cabling is broken with each repeat, this pattern does not create the thick, dense fabric characteristic of most cable patterns. Each small cross is embedded in the crotch of the tree above it, giving the fabric a bit more substance.

Yarn
Consumption: The twisting draws in the fabric, increasing yarn consumption substantially.

Suggested Uses: This pattern has a subtle quality; because of its broken cabling, it fades into the background stitches at the end of each repeat. Consider pairing it with an

2–12+

allover traveling-stitch pattern, such as a lattice, to give the effect of a tree growing up the side of a trellis or twigs scattered along the edge of the project.

Patterns: **FKC:** Sl 2 sts to cn and hold in front, k2, then k2 from cn.

BKC: Sl 2 sts to cn and hold in back, k2, then k2 from cn.

SFC: Sl 2 sts to cn and hold in front, p1, then k2 from cn.

SBC: Sl 1 st to cn and hold in back, k2, then p1 from cn.

SFKC: Sl 2 sts to cn and hold in front, k1, then k2 from cn.

SBKC: Sl 1 st to cn and hold in back, k2, then k1 from cn.

Tree Cable R (panel of 12 stitches)

ROW 1 (WS): P2, k2, p4, k2, p2.
ROW 2: SFC, p1, FKC, p1, SBC.
ROW 3: K1, p2, k1, p4, k1, p2, k1.
ROW 4: P1, SFC, k4, SBC, p1.
ROW 5: K2, p8, k2.
ROW 6: P2, SFKC, k2, SBKC, p2.
ROW 7: K3, p6, k3.
ROW 8: P3, SFKC, SBKC, p3.

Tree Cable L (panel of 12 stitches)

ROW 1 (WS): P2, k2, p4, k2, p2.
ROW 2: SFC, p1, FKC, p1, SBC.
ROW 3: K1, p2, k1, p4, k1, p2, k1.
ROW 4: P1, SFC, k4, SBC, p1.
ROW 5: K2, p8, k2.
ROW 6: P2, SFKC, k2, SBKC, p2.
ROW 7: K3, p6, k3.
ROW 8: P3, SFKC, SBKC, p3.

50. **ARROWHEAD CABLE**

Other Names:　Arrow cable, stacked spades.

General Description:　This pattern depicts stylized arrowheads with sharp points and rounded edges.

Properties:　Like other stacked cable patterns, the traveling lines do not cross so much as they blend into one another. However, there are enough crossed stitches to create a thicker fabric with enough structure to reduce its drape.

Yarn Consumption:　The crossed stitches draw in the fabric, increasing yarn consumption noticeably.

Suggested Uses:
\ 0–8

Arrowhead cables would work better as side panels than as center panels. On the side of a garment, they would give the appearance of drawing up from the middle; a cable in the center could give a garment the unfortunate appearance of drooping.

Pattern:

(panel of 24 stitches)

T4F: Sl 2 sts to cn and hold in front, p2, k2 from cn.
C2B: Sl 1 st to cn and hold in back, k1, k1 from cn.
T4B: Sl 2 sts to cn and hold in back, k2, p2 from cn.
C4B: Sl 2 sts to cn and hold in back, k2, k2 from cn.
T2F: Sl 1 st to cn and hold in front, p1, k1 from cn.
T2B: Sl 1 st to cn and hold in back, k1, p1 from cn.
C4F: Sl 2 sts to cn and hold in front, k2, k2 from cn.

ROW 1: K2, p4, T4F, p1, C2B, p1, T4B, p4, k2.
ROW 2: P2, k6, (p2, k1) twice, p2, k6, p2.
ROW 3: T4F, p4, T4F, T4B, p4, T4B.
ROW 4: K2, p2, k6, p4, k6, p2, k2.
ROW 5: P2, C4F, p4, T2F, T2B, p4, C4B, p2.
ROW 6: K2, p4, k5, p3, k5, p4, k2.
ROW 7: T4B, T4F, p3, C2B, p3, T4B, T4F.
ROW 8: P2, k4, (p2, k3) twice, p1, k4, p2.

51a–c.

THREE-STRAND BRAID

Other Names: Plait cable, branch cable.

General
Description: Braided cables are composed of three or more inter-twined bands and are thought to be inspired by the intricate patterns in traditional Celtic and Norse art. This basic three-strand cable is simple to work and makes a good introduction to braided cables.

Properties: This pattern resembles the braids commonly worn in hair and is formed by the intertwining of a third knit band through a simple cable. The strands are worked without any purl stitches between them, forming a thick, layered fabric. The cabling and the ribbing formed on either side of the pattern give it less of a horizontal spread than stockinette knit with the same number of stitches.

Yarn
Consumption: The cabling and ribbing draw in the fabric, increasing yarn consumption substantially.

Suggested Uses: The three-strand braid has a neat, even appearance that complements other rounded cable patterns, such as honeycomb and OXO cables, in sweater designs. Also try reducing the strand width to two stitches and cabling every other row to create a smaller, compact three-strand braid.

2–12+

Patterns: ***Three-Strand Braid L (panel of 13 stitches)***

ROW 1: P2, k9, p2.

ROW 2: K2, p9, k2.

ROW 3: P2, k3, sl next 3 sts to cn and hold in front; k3, then k3 from cn; p2.

ROWS 4 AND 6: Repeat Row 2.

ROW 5: Repeat Row 1.

ROW 7: P2, sl next 3 sts to cn and hold in back; k3, then k3 from cn; k3, p2.

ROW 8: Repeat Row 2.

***Three-Strand Braid R* (panel of 13 stitches)**

ROW 1: P2, k9, p2.

ROW 2: K2, p9, k2.

ROW 3: P2, sl next 3 sts to cn and hold in back; k3, then k3 from cn; k3, p2.

ROWS 4 AND 6: Repeat Row 2.

ROW 5: Repeat Row 1.

ROW 7: P2, k3, sl next 3 sts to cn and hold in front; k3, then k3 from cn; p2.

ROW 8: Repeat Row 2.

Variation: *Reverse Three-Strand Braid* (panel of 13 stitches)
The upside-down version of this pattern is useful to know when working a sweater from the top down.

ROWS 1: P2, k9, p2.

ROW 2: k2, p9, k2.

ROW 3: P2, sl next 3 sts to cn and hold in front; k3, then k3 from cn; k3, p2.

ROWS 4 AND 6: Repeat Row 2.

ROW 5: Repeat Row 1.

ROW 7: P2, k3, sl next 3 sts to cn and hold in back; k3, then k3 from cn; k3, p2.

52a–b.   **FOUR-STRAND BRAID**

Other Name: Aran braid.

General Description: With strands so crisply and compactly intertwined, this tightly braided pattern appears almost woven. Despite its complicated appearance, the pattern repeat is only four rows long, shorter than the simple cable and just as easy.

Properties: The tight cables resemble those of a standard shoelace. The dense patterning is balanced, and the entire panel is raised from a background of reverse stockinette in one bumpy block.

Yarn Consumption: The dense cabling draws in the fabric, increasing yarn consumption substantially.

Suggested Uses:
2–8

Not only does this dense, compact pattern add an intricate design element to winter sweaters, hats, or mittens, but its thickness provides warmth and a greater resistance to wind. These properties lend themselves to earmuff bands. Try knitting a band of four-strand braid about four-fifths of the circumference of the wearer's head, measured at the hairline and omitting the 2 selvage stitches on either side; add a few inches of garter stitch at the end to create horizontal ribbing; and join at the ends.

Pattern:

(panel of 12 stitches)

ROWS 1 AND 3 (WS): K2, p8, k2.
ROW 2: P2, (sl 2 sts to cn and hold in back, k2, then k2 from cn) twice, p2.
ROW 4: P2, k2, sl 2 sts to cn and hold in front, k2, then k2 from cn, k2, p2.

Variation:

Five-Strand Aran Braid (panel of 14 stitches)
With the same dense, compact interweaving as the four-strand version, this pattern adds a strand and crosses twice every other row.

ROWS 1 AND 3 (WS): K2, p10, k2.
ROW 2: P2, (sl 2 sts to cn and hold in back, k2, then k2 from cn) twice, k2, p2.
ROW 4: P2, k2, (sl 2 sts to cn and hold in front, k2, then k2 from cn, k2) twice, p2.

53.   **FIVE-STRAND BRAID**

Other Name: Celtic princess braid.

General
Description: Though this five-strand braid has essentially the same
construction as the five-strand Aran braid, its curvy edges
and even tension make it look more like the simple
three-strand braid. The strands create a complex woven
plaiting that makes it difficult to count the strands,
but careful inspection will prove the number to be five.

Properties: Single purl stitches are inserted between the strands
↔   and the pattern is worked over eight rows, giving this
fabric greater horizontal stretch and a loosened drape
compared to its Aran relations.

Yarn
Consumption: The ribbing and multiple cable crossings draw in the
fabric, increasing yarn consumption substantially.

Suggested Uses: This braid would be a wonderful sleeve adornment on
＼2–12+   a sturdy raglan sweater or cardigan—with a bit of
simple math, the cable could be designed to blend
organically into ribbing around the neck.

Pattern: **(panel of 18 stitches)**

BC: Sl 3 sts to cn and hold in back, k2, then sl the
purl st from cn back to LH needle and purl it, then
k2 from cn.

FC: Sl 3 sts to cn and hold in front, k2, then sl the purl st from cn back to LH needle and purl it, then k2 from cn.

ROW 1 (WS) AND ALL OTHER WRONG-SIDE ROWS: K2, (p2, k1) 4 times, p2, k2.
ROW 2: P2, (k2, p1) 4 times, k2, p2.
ROW 4: P2, k2, (p1, FC) twice, p2.
ROW 6: Repeat Row 2.
ROW 8: P2, (BC, p1) twice, k2, p2.

54.

OPEN THREE-STRAND BRAID

General Description:

This rambling, three-strand braid is often found on commercially produced Aran sweaters because its simple patterning fills a large area. The beginning knitter may want to borrow this tactic and make liberal use of this pattern when attempting an Aran-style sweater for the first time.

Properties:

Two purl stitches separate each strand to give this fabric a loose drape with a tendency to stretch. Repeats are stretched over twelve rows; each strand turns into a straight runway between cable crossings, which gives the overall patterning a geometric look.

Yarn
Consumption:

Though the multiple cable crossings and ribbing draw in the fabric, the open areas and additional rows partially mitigate this effect, increasing yarn consumption noticeably but not substantially.

Suggested Uses:

2–12+

In addition to its role as a beginner's Aran, the open three-strand braid would be quick and stylish if knit as an allover pattern for a large shoulder bag, especially if a bulky-weight yarn is used.

Pattern:

(panel of 14 stitches)

BC: Sl 4 sts to cn and hold in back, k2, sl the 2 purl sts from cn back to LH and purl them, then k2 from cn.

FC: Sl 4 sts to cn and hold in front, k2, sl the 2 purl sts from cn back to LH and purl them, then k2 from cn.

ROW 1: P2, (k2, p2) 3 times.

ROW 2 AND ALL OTHER EVEN-NUMBERED ROWS: K2, (p2, k2) 3 times.

ROW 3: P2, BC, p2, k2, p2.

ROWS 5 AND 7: Repeat Row 1.

ROW 9: P2, k2, p2, FC, p2.

ROWS 11 AND 12: Repeat Rows 1 and 2.

55. **OPEN FOUR-STRAND BRAID**

General
Description:

This pattern is formed by four undulating strands that converge at a central point before curving out to the edges of the fabric and repeating the process.

Properties:

Despite the purl stitches separating the strands, this pattern creates a structured fabric prone to stiffness; however, rounded edges soften its appearance.

Yarn
Consumption:

The multiple cable crossings create a thick, layered fabric and increase yarn consumption considerably.

Suggested Uses:

2–12+

The balanced patterning makes this open braid appropriate as a center panel down the front of an intricate Aran-style sweater, although it would also look excellent knit up the front edges of a cardigan and extended up around a hood.

Pattern:

(panel of 24 stitches)

FC: Sl 3 sts to cn and hold in front, k3, then k3 from cn.
BC: Sl 3 sts to cn and hold in back, k3, then k3 from cn.
SFC: Sl 3 sts to cn and hold in front, p1, then k3 from cn.
SBC: Sl 1 st to cn and hold in back, k3, then p1 from cn.

ROW 1 (WS): K2, p3, k4, p6, k4, p3, k2.
ROW 2: P2, k3, p4, k6, p4, k3, p2.

ROW 3 AND ALL SUBSEQUENT WRONG-SIDE ROWS:
Knit all knit sts and purl all purl sts.
ROW 4: P2, (SFC, p2 SBC) twice, p2.
ROW 6: P3, SFC, SBC, p2, SFC, SBC, p3.
ROW 8: P4, FC, p4, BC, p4.
ROW 10: P3, SBC, SFC, p2, SBC, SFC, p3.
ROW 12: P2, (SBC, p2 SFC) twice, p2.
ROW 14: P2, k3, p4, BC, p4, k3, p2.
ROWS 16 AND 18: Repeat Rows 4 and 6.
ROW 20: P4, FC, p4, FC, p4.
ROWS 22 AND 24: Repeat Rows 10 and 12.

56.   **OPEN FIVE-STRAND BRAID**

Other Name: Hartshorn cable.

General
Description: This pattern creates an impressive tangle of strands that
each burst into the open and then sharply turn back
into the fray. Three of the five strands take turns forming a straight line down the center, giving the pattern
a stark, strong appearance, like a mythical dagger
struck into the ground.

Properties: The ensnarled bands give this fabric some structure,
though the ebb and flow of its outlines give it more
drape than a simple cable pattern. The purl stitches
separating each band give the fabric some stretch,

though any ribbing is broken by the traveling bands, keeping it from drawing in on itself drastically.

Yarn Consumption:

🪢🪢🪢🪢🪢

The multiple cable crossings create a thick, layered fabric and increase yarn consumption considerably.

Suggested Uses:

2–10

The unusual threading would make this a striking center panel on any cabled sweater or central motif on any project designed to draw the eye. Try pairing it with upward-pointing broken cables, perhaps worked with bobbles at the points to emphasize the upward thrust of two of this pattern's strands.

Pattern:

(panel of 28 stitches)

FC: Sl 2 sts to cn and hold in front, p2, then k2 from cn.
FKC: Same as FC but knit all 4 sts.
BC: Sl 2 sts to cn and hold in back, k2, then p2 from cn.
BKC: Same as BC but knit all 4 sts.
SBC: Sl 1 st to cn and hold in back, k2, then p1 from cn.

ROWS 1 AND 3 (WS): K9, p10, k9.
ROW 2: P9, BKC, k2, FKC, p9.
ROW 4: P7, BC, k2, BKC, FC, p7.
ROW 5 AND ALL OTHER WRONG-SIDE ROWS: Knit all knit sts and purl all purl sts.
ROW 6: P5, BC, p1, SBC, k2, SFC, p1, FC, p5.
ROW 8: P3, BC, p2, SBC, p1, k2, p1, SFC, p2, FC, p3.
ROW 10: P3, k2, p3, SBC, p2, k2, p2, SFC, p3, k2, p3.

ROW 12: P3, FC, SBC, p3, k2, p3, SFC, BC, p3.
ROW 14: P5, BKC, p4, k2, p4, FKC, p5.
ROW 16: P3, BC, FC, p2, k2, p2, BC, FC, p3.
ROW 18: P3, k2, p4, FC, k2, BC, p4, k2, p3.
ROW 20: P3, FC, p4, FKC, k2, p4, BC, p3.
ROW 22: P5, FC, p2, k2, BKC, p2, BC, p5.
ROW 24: P7, FC, FKC, k2, BC, p7.

57a–b. 📷 **TWISTED-STITCH WAVES**

General
Description:

A twisted-stitch pattern in the Bavarian tradition, this pattern uses the simple technique of knitting stitches out of order to cause a single line of knit stitches to move across the fabric.

Properties:

The simple, waving pattern is made up of a few knit stitches raised against a bed of reverse stockinette. The waves are too far away from one another to cause any appreciable ribbing; the resulting fabric has very similar characteristics to reverse stockinette.

Yarn
Consumption:

With knit stitches only occasionally breaking the surface of reverse stockinette, this pattern uses approximately the same amount of yarn as stockinette.

Suggested Uses:
2–10

The meandering lines give this pattern a casual look; try it with a mercerized cotton for a simple, curvy summer tank.

Pattern: **(multiple of 8 stitches + 2)**

📺

RT: Skip 1 st and knit the 2nd st, leave on needle; then purl the skipped st, drop both sts from needle together.

LT: Skip 1 st and purl into back of 2nd st, leave on needle; then knit the skipped st, drop both sts from needle together.

ROW 1 (WS): K1, * k7, p1; rep from *, end k1.
ROW 2: P1, * LT, p6; rep from *, end p1.
ROW 3 AND ALL SUBSEQUENT WS ROWS: Knit all knit sts and purl all purl sts.
ROW 4: P1, * p1, LT, p5; rep from *, end p1.
ROW 6: P1, * p2, LT, p4; rep from *, end p1.
ROW 8: P1, * p3, LT, p3; rep from *, end p1.
ROW 10: P1, * p4, LT, p2; rep from *, end p1.
ROW 12: P1, * p5, LT, p1; rep from *, end p1.
ROW 14: P1, * p6, LT; rep from *, end p1.
ROW 16: P1, * p7, k1, p6; rep from *, end p1.
ROW 18: P1, * p6, RT; rep from *, end p1.
ROW 20: P1, * p5, RT, p1; rep from *, end p1.
ROW 22: P1, * p4, RT, p2; rep from *, end p1.
ROW 24: P1, * p3, RT, p3; rep from *, end p1.
ROW 26: P1, * p2, RT, p4; rep from *, end p1.
ROW 28: P1, * p1, RT, p5; rep from *, end p1.
ROW 30: P1, * RT, p6; rep from *, end p1.
ROW 32: P1, * k1, p7; rep from *, end k1.

Variation:

Traveling Line Waves (multiple of 6 stitches + 2)

In this version, the lines are closer together and thicker, similar to the bands in open braids.

BC: Sl 1 st to cn, hold in back, k2, p1 from cn.
FC: Sl 2 sts to cn, hold in front, p1, k2 from cn.

ROW 1: P1, * p3, BC; rep from *, end p1.
ROW 2 AND ALL SUBSEQUENT EVEN-NUMBERED
   ROWS: Knit all knit sts and purl all purl sts.
ROW 3: P1, * p2, BC, p1; rep from *, end p1.
ROW 5: P1, * p1, BC, p2; rep from *, end p1.
ROW 7: P1, * BC, p3; rep from *, end p1.
ROW 9: P1, * FC, p3; rep from *, end p1.
ROW 11: P1, * p1, FC, p2; rep from *, end p1.
ROW 13: P1, * p2, FC, p1; rep from *, end p1.
ROW 15: P1, * p3, FC; rep from *, end p1.
ROW 16: See Row 2.

58.

TWISTED-STITCH DIAMONDS

General
Description:

These graceful, swooping diamonds build on the twisted-stitch wave pattern—they are formed by two opposite waves placed atop each other, crossing halfway across the panel.

Properties: The raised knit stitches across a field of reverse stockinette do not create any appreciable ribbing and give this fabric a drape and feel similar to reverse stockinette.

Yarn Consumption: Without enough knit stitches to draw in the fabric significantly, this pattern uses approximately the same amount of yarn as stockinette.

Suggested Uses: Consider knitting this pattern with very small needles and in conjunction with other twisted-stitch patterns to create intricate Bavarian stockings. Also try replacing the center diamond with bobbles or a seed stitch filling.

Pattern: **(panel of 14 stitches)**

RT: Skip 1 st and knit the 2nd st, leave on needle; then purl the skipped st, drop both sts from needle together.

LT: Skip 1 st and purl into back of 2nd st, leave on needle; then knit the skipped st, drop both sts from needle together.

ROW 1: P6, * skip 1 st and knit the 2nd st, leave on needle; then knit the skipped st, sl both sts from needle together *, p6.

ROW 2: K6, p2, k6.

ROW 3: P5, RT, LT, p5.

ROW 4: K5, p1, k2, p1, k5.

ROW 5: P4, RT, p2 LT, p4.

ROW **6:** K4, p1, k4, p1, k4.

ROW **7:** P3, RT, p1, repeat from * to * of Row 1, p1, LT, p3.

ROW **8:** K3, p1, k2, p2, k2, p1, k3.

ROW **9:** P2, RT, p1, RT, LT, p1, LT, p2.

ROW **10:** (K2, p1) 4 times, k2.

ROW **11:** P1, RT, p1, RT, p2, LT, p1, LT, p1.

ROW **12:** K1, p1, k2, p1, k4, p1, k2, p1, k1.

ROW **13:** P1, k1, p2, k1, p4, k1, p2, k1, p1.

ROWS **14, 16, 18, 20, 22, AND 24:** Repeat Rows 12, 10, 8, 6, 4, and 2.

ROW **15:** P1, LT, p1, LT, p2, RT, p1, RT, p1.

ROW **17:** P2, LT, p1, LT, RT, p1, RT, p2.

ROW **19:** P3, LT, p1, repeat from * to * of Row 1, p1, RT, p3.

ROW **21:** P4, LT, p2 RT, p4.

ROW **23:** P5, LT, RT, p5.

59a–b.

TWISTED-STITCH LATTICE

General Description:

Crisp, parallel twisted-stitch lines cross repeatedly to form a lattice of stacked diamonds. Though similar in motif to the slip-stitch trellis, this construction is very different.

Properties:

The lattice of twisted stitches stabilizes the fabric, giving it less stretch and drape than stockinette.

Yarn
Consumption:

Without enough knit stitches to draw in the fabric significantly, this pattern uses approximately the same amount of yarn as stockinette.

Suggested Uses:

00–6

The crisp design makes this pattern a nice choice for a wide front panel down the front of a formal sweater. It would also be a simple way to add interest to a cushion or afghan. Avoid projects that require shaping over the pattern—increasing or decreasing without distortion would be difficult.

Pattern:

(multiple of 8 stitches + 2)

RT: Skip 1 st and knit the 2nd st, leave on needle; then purl the skipped st, drop both sts from needle together.

LT: Skip 1 st and purl into back of 2nd st, leave on needle; then knit the skipped st, drop both sts from needle together.

ROW 1 (WS): K4, * p2, k6; rep from *, end last repeat k4.

ROW 2: P3, * RT, LT, p4; rep from *, end last repeat p3.

ROW 3: K3, * p1, k2, p1, k4; rep from *, end last repeat k3.

ROW 4: P2, * RT, p2, LT, p2; rep from *.

ROW 5: K2, * p1, k4, p1, k2; rep from *.

ROW 6: P1, * RT, p4, LT; rep from *, end p1.

ROW 7: K1, * p1, k6, p1; rep from *, end k1.

ROW 8: P1, k1, * p6, skip 1 st and knit the 2nd st, then knit the skipped st through back loop, sl both sts from needle together; rep from *, end p6, k1, p1.

ROWS 9, 11, 13, AND 15: Repeat Row 7, 5, 3, and 1.

ROW 10: P1, * LT, p4, RT; rep from *, end p1.

ROW 12: P2, * LT, p2, RT, p2; rep from *.

ROW 14: P3, * LT, RT, p4; rep from *, end last repeat p3.

ROW 16: P4, * skip 1 st and knit the 2nd st, then knit the skipped st through back loop, sl both sts from needle together; p6; rep from *, end last repeat p4.

Variation: *Aran Lattice* or *Traveling Line Diamonds* (multiple of 12 stitches + 14)
So named for its bulky affinity to Aran-style cables and honeycombs, this pattern could just as easily be called traveling lines lattice. Its thick bands are similar to those found in traveling line waves.

FC: Sl 2 sts to cn and hold in front, p2, then k2 from cn.

BC: Sl 2 sts to cn and hold in back, k2, then p2 from cn.

FKC: Sl 2 sts to cn and hold in front, k2, then k2 from cn.

BKC: Sl 2 sts to cn and hold in back, k2, then k2 from cn.

ROW 1: P3, BC, FC, *p4, BC, FC; rep from * to last 3 sts, p3.

ROW 2: K3, p2, *k4, p2; rep from * to last 3 sts, k3.

ROW 3: P1, BC, p4, FC; rep from * to last st, p1.

ROW 4: K1, p2, k8, * p4, k8; rep from * to last 3 sts, p2, k1.

ROW 5: P1, k2, p8, * BKC, p8; rep from * to last 3 sts, k2, p1.

ROW 6: Repeat Row 4.

ROW 7: P1, *FC, p4, BC; rep from * to last st, p1.

ROW 8: Repeat Row 2.

ROW 9: P3, FC, BC, * p4, FC, BC; rep from * to last 3 sts, p3.

ROW 10: K5, p4, * k8, p4; rep from * to last 5 sts, k5.

ROW 11: P5, FKC, * p8, FKC; rep from * to last 5 sts, p5.

ROW 12: Repeat Row 10.

60.

TRAVELING LINE WHORL

General Description:

This fun pattern introduces a technique essential to knitting Celtic knot cables: the work 5 tog, which makes the cable appear to turn around on itself. In this pattern, it creates a simple side twirl.

Properties:

Traveling knit lines on a bed of reverse stockinette create an embossed fabric with some structure, reducing its stretch and drape.

Yarn
Consumption:

Suggested Uses:
2–10

The raised crossings draw in the fabric and increase yarn consumption.

The vertical scroll of this pattern cries out to be used in edgings and bands. An Aran panel would be an obvious use, or try this stitch along the edge of a bedspread or alone as a wristband.

Pattern:

(panel of 22 stitches)

BC: Sl 2 sts to cn and hold in back, k2, then p2 from cn.

BKC: Sl 2 sts to cn and hold in back, k2, then k2 from cn.

FC: Sl 2 sts to cn and hold in front, p2, then k2 from cn.

FKC: Sl 2 sts to cn and hold in front, k2, then k2 from cn.

M3: (K1, p1, k1) all into the next stitch.

WORK 5 TOG: With yarn in back, sl 3 sts purlwise, * pass 2nd st on RH needle over 1st (center) st, slip center st back to LH needle, pass 2nd st on LH needle over *, slip center st back to RH needle; rep from * to * once more, purl center st. (Note: Stitch referred to as "center" stitch is center one of 5 sts.)

ROW 1: BC, p1, FC, BC, p9.
ROW 2: K11, p4, k5, p2.
ROW 3: K2, p5, BKC, p11.

ROW 4: Repeat Row 2.
ROW 5: FC, p1, BC, FC, p9.
ROW 6: K9, p2, k4, p2, k1, p2, k2.
ROW 7: P2, work 5 tog, p4, FC, p4, M1, M3, M1, p2.
ROW 8: K2, p2, k1, p2, k4, p2, k9.
ROW 9: P9, FC, BC, p1, FC.
ROW 10: P2, k5, p4, k11.
ROW 11: P11, FKC, p5, k2.
ROW 12: Repeat Row 10.
ROW 13: P9, BC, FC, p1, BC.
ROW 14: Repeat Row 8.
ROW 15: P2, M1, M3, M1, p4, BC, p4, work 5 tog, p2.
ROW 16: Repeat Row 6.

61. 📷 **TRAVELING LINE DOUBLE HELIX**

General
Description:

Though this pattern predates the modern scientific field of microbiology, most people associate the double helix with the structure of DNA. However, the name simply refers to a pair of lines spiraling around a common axis.

Properties:

Raised knit bands swirl around each other and repeatedly cross on a bed of reverse stockinette, creating a structured fabric with limited drape.

Yarn
Consumption:

The raised crossings draw in the fabric and increase yarn consumption, particularly if the panel is repeated.

Suggested Uses: This narrow panel will add lengthy curves to vertical
      2–10   strip. Consider knitting a wine-bottle cozy with this
               as a central, singular motif to add a special touch to a
               hostess gift.

Pattern: **(panel of 9 stitches)**

BC: Sl 2 sts to cn and hold in back, k2, then p2 from
      cn.
BKC: Sl 2 sts to cn and hold in back, k2, then k2
      from cn.
FC: Sl 2 sts to cn and hold in front, p2, then k2 from
      cn.
FKC: Sl 2 sts to cn and hold in front, k2, then k2
      from cn.
SBC: Sl 1 st to cn and hold in back, p1, then k2 from cn.
SFC: Sl 2 sts to cn and hold in front, k2, then p1
      from cn.

ROW 1: P3, BC, k2,
ROW 2: P2, k2, p2, k3.
ROW 3: P1, BC, p1, SBC
ROW 4: K1, p2, k3, p2, k1.
ROW 5: SBC, p1, BC, p1.
ROW 6: K3, p2, k2, p2.
ROW 7: K2, BC, p3.
ROW 8: K5, p4.
ROW 9: BKC, p5.
ROWS 10, 12, 14, AND 16: Repeat Rows 8, 6, 4, and 2.

ROW 11: K2, FC, p3.
ROW 13: SFC, p1, FC, p1.
ROW 15: P1, FC, p1, SFC
ROW 17: P3, FC, k2.
ROW 18: P4, k5.
ROW 19: P5, BKC.
ROW 20: P4, k5.

62a–b.

RIBBED CABLE

General
Description:

These cables are actually two paired twisted-stitch lines that cross at regular intervals. Ribbed cables are frequently found in intricately patterned Bavarian stockings.

Properties:
◄►

This pattern creates a thick, structured fabric with substantial lateral elasticity.

Yarn
Consumption:

The ribbing within the cables draws the fabric in even more than plain cables, increasing yarn consumption substantially.

Suggested Uses:
00–6

The ribbings give this pattern stretch and cushion, making it ideal for socks. Because twisted-stitch patterns look neater when knit on smaller needles, try this pattern on any small, intricate project, such as fancy winter gloves for special occasions.

Patterns: ***Ribbed Cable L** (panel of 11 stitches)*

ROW 1 (WS): K2, (p1 tbl, k1) 3 times, p1 tbl, k2.
ROW 2: P2, sl 3 sts to cn and hold in front, (k1 tbl, p1) twice on next 4 sts, then from cn k1 tbl, p1, k1 tbl the 3 sts, p2.
ROWS 3, 5, 7, AND 9: Repeat Row 1.
ROWS 4, 6, 8, AND 10: P2, (k1 tbl, p1) 3 times, k1 tbl, p2.

***Ribbed Cable R** (panel of 11 stitches)*

ROW 1 (WS): K2, (p1 tbl, k1) 3 times, p1 tbl, k2.
ROW 2: P2, sl next 4 sts to cn and hold in back, k1 tbl, p1, k1 tbl on next 3 sts, then from cn (p1, k1 tbl) twice, p2.
ROWS 3, 5, 7, AND 9: Repeat Row 1.
ROWS 4, 6, 8, AND 10: P2, (k1 tbl, p1) 3 times, k1 tbl, p2.

63. **WAVING BRANCHES**

Other Name: Interlocking faggoted cables.

General Description: This unique cable pattern is a complicated braiding of stockinette strands that fan out into a classic faggoting pattern before recombining into a solid trunk of classic 4x4 cable. The swirling combination of traditional techniques is fascinating to view and work.

Properties:
↔

The elastic fabric has raised elements at each cable crossing. The cables give the fabric structure, although the large areas of openwork also give it excellent drape.

Yarn
Consumption:

Unlike most cable patterns, this stitch's large areas of faggoting open up the fabric and mitigate the increased yarn usage of its cable crossings, decreasing yarn consumption overall.

Suggested Uses:
00–12

This pattern's mesmerizing hourglass patterning would make for a flattering lace top to be worn over a camisole or tank top. Also try it for a stunning and unusual wrap.

Pattern:

(multiple of 16 stitches)

C8P: Sl 4 sts to cn and hold in front, p4, p4 sts from cn.
C8K: Sl 4 sts to cn and hold in front, k4, k4 sts from cn.

ROWS 1, 3, 5, 7, 9, AND 11: * (Yo, k2tog) 4 times, k8; rep from *.
ROWS 2 AND 4: Purl.
ROW 6: * C8P, p8; rep from *.
ROWS 8 AND 10: Purl.
ROWS 12, 14, 16, AND 18: * (P2tog, yo) 4 times, p8; rep from *.
ROWS 13 AND 15: Knit.
ROW 17: * C8K, k8; rep from *.

ROWS 19 AND 21: Knit.

ROW 22: See Row 12.

64a–b.

SIMPLE SPLIT CABLE

Other Name: Linked lattice.

General
Description:
In this pattern, traveling bands cross and split like endless interlocking arms swirling around each other at a dance. Despite its many rows, this pattern is as easy to work as a simple cable once the pattern reveals itself in the fabric.

Properties: The cables split wide enough for this fabric to retain some drape, though the allover embossed cable pattern gives the fabric a structured feel.

Yarn
Consumption:
The cables draw in the fabric without causing any significant ribbing, increasing yarn consumption noticeably but not substantially.

Suggested Uses:
2–8
Though another handsome choice for a sweater, if this pattern's fabric is turned on its side, the linked lattice resembles a clothes-drying rack or stacks of flying saucers. Be creative in its application—perhaps it would be just right as a pillow in a child's room or a cushion for the laundry-room chair.

Pattern: **(multiple of 12 stitches + 14)**

T3B: Sl 1 st to cn and hold in back, k2, then p1 from cn.

T3F: Sl 2 sts to cn and hold in front, p1, then k2 from cn.

C4F: Sl 2 sts to cn and hold in front, k2, then k2 from cn.

C4B: Sl 2 sts to cn and hold in back, k2, then k2 from cn.

ROW 1: P5, k4, * p8, k4, rep from * to last 5 sts, p5.

ROW 2: K5, p4, * k8, p4, rep from * to last 5 sts, k5.

ROW 3: P5, C4F, * p8, C4F; rep from * to last 5 sts, p5.

ROW 4: Repeat Row 2.

ROW 5: P4, T3B, T3F, * p6, T3B, T3F; rep from * to last 4 sts, p4.

ROW 6: K4, p2, k2, p2, * k6, p2, k2, p2; rep from * to last 4 sts, k4.

ROW 7: P3, T3B, p2, T3F, * p4, T3B, p2, T3F; rep from * to last 3 sts, p3.

ROW 8: K3, p2, * k4, p2; rep from * to last 3 sts, k3.

ROW 9: * P2, T3B, p4, T3F; rep from * to last 2 sts, p2.

ROW 10: * K2, p2, k6, p2; rep from * to last 2 sts, k2.

ROW 11: P1, * T3B, p6, T3F; rep from * to last st, p1.

ROW 12: K1, p2, k8, * p4, k8; rep from * to last 3 sts, p2, k1.

ROW 13: P1, k2, p8, * C4F, p8; rep from * to last 3 sts, k2, p1.

ROW 14: Repeat Row 12.

ROW 15: P1, k2, p8, * k4, p8; rep from * to last 3 sts, k2, p1.

ROWS 16, 17, AND 18: Repeat Rows 12, 13, and then Row 12 again.

ROW 19: P1, * T3F, p6, T3B; rep from * to last st, p1.

ROW 20: Repeat Row 10.

ROW 21: * P2, T3F, p4, T3B; rep from * to last 2 sts, p2.

ROW 22: Repeat Row 8.

ROW 23: P3, T3F, p2, T3B, * p4, T3F, p2, T3B; rep from * to last 3 sts, p3.

ROW 24: Repeat Row 6.

ROW 25: P4, T3F, T3B * p6, T3F, T3B; rep from * to last 4 sts, p4.

ROWS 26–28: Repeat Rows 2–3, and then Row 2 again.

To reverse the direction of the cable crossing, replace C4F with C4B.

Variation: *Interlocking Lattice* (multiple of 6 stitches + 2)
If each side of the twisted-stitch lattice were pushed together, the side corners of each diamond would overlap, which is exactly what this pattern looks like.

FC: Sl 1 st to cn and hold in front, p1, then k1 from cn.

BC: Sl 1 st to cn and hold in back, k1, then p1 from cn.

FKC: Sl 1 st to cn and hold in front, k1, then k1
from cn.

BKC: Sl 1 st to cn and hold in back, k1, then k1
from cn.

ROW 1 (WS): K1, p1, * k4, p2; rep from *, end last
repeat k4, p1, k1.

ROW 2: P1, * FC, p2, BC; rep from *, end p1.

ROW 3 AND ALL SUBSEQUENT WRONG-SIDE ROWS:
Knit all knit sts and purl all purl sts.

ROW 4: P2, * FC, BC, p2; rep from *.

ROW 6: P3, * BKC, p4; rep from *, end last repeat p3.

ROW 8: P2, * BC, FC, p2; rep from *.

ROWS 10, 12, AND 14: Repeat rows 4, 6, and 8.

ROW 16: P1, * BC, p2, FC; rep from *, end p1.

ROW 18: BC, p4, * FKC, p4; rep from *, end FC.

ROW 20: K1, p4, * BC, FC, p2; rep from *, end p2,
k1.

ROW 22: K1, p4, * FC, BC, p2; rep from *, end p2,
k1.

ROW 24: FC, p4, * FKC, p4; rep from *, end BC.

65a–b.

GARTER STITCH CABLE

General
Description:

This pattern is interesting because it cables two bands
knit in different stitch patterns—one in garter stitch and
one in stockinette. The pattern is outlined best when
worked against a background of reverse stockinette.

Properties: The garter-stitch band appears shadowed, giving this
               pattern a three-dimensional quality as well as a softness
               that simple stockinette cables lack.

Yarn   The cabling draws in the fabric, increasing yarn
Consumption: consumption noticeably.

Suggested Uses: This pattern's layered effect would give a garment a
    0–6   modern feel when used in place of a simple cable.
               Try three panels side-by-side to create a scarf with
               unusual depth.

Patterns: ***Garter Stitch Cable R* (panel of 8 stitches)**

             ROW 1: K8.
             ROW 2: P4, k4.
             ROWS 3–6: (Rep Rows 1 and 2) twice.
             ROW 7: Sl 4 sts to cn and hold in back, k4, knit 4 sts
                 from cn.
             ROW 8: K4, p4.
             ROW 9: K8.
             ROWS 10–18: (Rep Rows 8 and 9) 4 times, then
                 repeat Row 8.
             ROW 19: Repeat Row 7.
             ROW 20: P4, k4.
             ROW 21: K8.
             ROWS 22 AND 23: Repeat Rows 20 and 21.
             ROW 24: Repeat Row 20.

Garter Stitch Cable L (panel of 8 stitches)

ROW 1: K8.

ROW 2: P4, k4.

ROWS 3–6: (Rep Rows 1 and 2) twice.

ROW 7: Sl 4 sts to cn and hold in front, k4, knit 4 sts from cn.

ROW 8: K4, p4.

ROW 9: K8.

ROWS 10–18: (Rep Rows 8 and 9) 4 times, then repeat Row 8.

ROW 19: Repeat Row 7.

ROW 20: P4, k4.

ROW 21: K8.

ROWS 22 AND 23: Repeat Rows 20 and 21.

ROW 24: Repeat Row 20.

66a–b.

MOSS-STITCH LATTICE

General
Description:

This highly textured pattern is a fancy version of the Aran lattice, with a small variation in the crossings: Adding reverse crosses on the wrong side creates the impression that each traveling line splits at the crossing and merges into the next line.

Properties:

This pattern creates a dense, embossed fabric with more cushion than stretch. It will add bulk and structure to a garment while stripping away its tendency to drape.

Yarn
Consumption:

Suggested Uses:

Pattern:

Both the moss-stitch filling and the crossings draw in the fabric, increasing yarn consumption significantly.

This structured pattern's rugged texture would make for a very handsome sweater and add considerable interest to a sweater knit in a single color.

(multiple of 14 stitches + 13)

BC: Sl 1 to cn and hold in back, k2, then p1 from cn.

FC: Sl 2 sts to cn and hold in front, p1, then k2 from cn.

RBC: Sl 2 sts to cn and hold in back, p1, then sl the knit st from cn back to LH needle and knit it, then p1 from cn.

RFC: Sl 2 sts to cn and hold in front, p1, then sl the knit st from cn back to LH needle and knit it, then p1 from cn.

ROW 1 (WS): P2, * (k1, p1) 5 times, RBC, p1; rep from *, end (k1, p1) 4 times, k1, p2.

ROW 2: FC, (p1, k1) 3 times, p1, BC, * k1, FC, (p1, k1) 3 times, p1, BC; rep from *.

ROWS 3, 5, AND 7: Knit all knit sts and purl all purl sts.

ROW 4: K1, FC, (p1, k1) twice, p1, BC, k1, * p1, k1, FC, (p1, k1) twice, p1, BC, k1; rep from *.

ROW 6: P1, k1, FC, p1, k1, p1, BC, k1, p1, * k1, p1, k1, FC, p1, k1, p1, BC, k1, p1; rep from *.

ROW 8: K1, p1, k1, FC, p1, BC, k1, p1, k1, * (p1, k1) twice, FC, p1, BC, k1, p1, k1; rep from *.

ROW 9: (P1, k1) twice, * p1, RFC, (p1, k1) 5 times; rep from *, end p1, RFC, p1, (k1, p1) twice.

ROW 10: P1, k1, p1, BC, k1, FC, p1, k1, p1, * (k1, p1) twice, BC, k1, FC, p1, k1, p1; rep from *

ROWS 11, 13, AND 15: Knit all knit sts and purl all purl sts.

ROW 12: K1, p1, BC, k1, p1, k1, FC, p1, k1, * P1, k1, p1, BC, k1, p1, k1, FC, p1, k1; rep from *.

ROW 14: P1, BC, (k1, p1) twice, k1, FC, p1, * k1, p1, BC, (k1, p1) twice, k1, FC, p1; rep from *.

ROW 16: BC, (k1, p1) 3 times, k1, FC, * p1, BC, (k1, p1) 3 times, k1, FC; rep from *.

Variation: *Double Moss-Stitch Lattice* (multiple of 14 stitches + 15)
In this version, the moss-stitch filling is replaced with double moss stitch and alternates with a stockinette fill every other row of diamonds, giving this pattern the feel of textured argyle.

FC: Sl 2 sts to cn and hold in front, k1, then k2 from cn.

BC: Sl 1 st to cn and hold in back, k2, then k1 from cn.

C5B: Sl 1 st to cn and hold in back, k4, then p1 from cn.

ROW 1: K4, BC, p1, FC, * k7, BC, p1, FC; rep from * to last 4 sts, k4.

ROW 2: P7, k1, * p13, k1; rep from * to last 7 sts, p7.

ROW 3: K3, BC, p1, k1, p1, FC, * k5, BC, p1, k1,
p1, FC; rep from * to last 3 sts, k3.

ROW 4: P6, k1, p1, k1, * p11, k1, p1, k1; rep from *
to last 6 sts, p6.

ROW 5: K2, BC, p1, (k1, p1) twice, FC, * k3, BC,
p1, (k1, p1) twice, FC; rep from * to last 2 sts, k2.

ROW 6: P5, k1, (p1, k1) twice, * p9, k1, (p1, k1)
twice; rep from * to last 5 sts, p5.

ROW 7: K1, * BC, p1, (k1, p1) 3 times, FC, k1; rep
from * to end.

ROW 8: P4, k1, (p1, k1) 3 times, * p7, k1, (p1, k1) 3
times; rep from * to last 4 sts, p4.

ROW 9: K3, p1, (k1, p1) 4 times, * C5B, p1, (k1, p1)
4 times; rep from * to last 3 sts, k3.

ROW 10: P3, k1, (p1, k1) 4 times, * p5, k1, (p1, k1)
4 times; rep from * to last 3 sts, p3.

ROW 11: K1, * FC, p1, (k1, p1) 3 times, BC, k1; rep
from * to end.

ROW 12: Repeat Row 8.

ROW 13: K2, FC, p1, (k1, p1) twice, BC, * k3, FC,
p1, (k1, p1) twice, BC; rep from * to last 2 sts, k2.

ROWS 14, 16, AND 18: Repeat rows 6, 4, and 2.

ROW 15: K3, FC, p1, k1, p1, BC, * k5, FC, p1, k1,
p1, BC; rep from * to last 3 sts, k3.

ROW 17: K4, FC, p1, BC, * k7, FC, p1, BC; rep
from * to last 4 sts, k4.

ROW 19: K5, C5B, * k9, C5B; rep from * to last 5 sts, k5.

ROW 20: Purl.

67a–b.

MOSS-STITCH DIAMONDS

Other Names: Moss-stitch double helix.

General Description: Unlike its lattice cousin, this pattern forms a single strip of moss-stitch-filled diamonds bordered by twisted-stitch lines on a background of reverse stockinette. It is an understated Aran-style panel, with a touch of the subtlety usually reserved for gansey patterns.

Properties: This pattern forms a lightly textured, relatively flat fabric, which retains a fair amount of drape.

Yarn Consumption: The single-stitch crossings and moss-stitch filling draw in the fabric only marginally. Over a single repeat, this pattern will use approximately the same amount of yarn as stockinette. The marginal differences will start to accumulate over multiple repeats, so plan accordingly.

Suggested Uses: The delicate yet crisp patterning begs to be showcased— perhaps worked on one side down the front of a skirt or down one side of a sweater blouse.

\ 2–8

Pattern: **(panel of 11 stitches)**

BC: Sl 1 st to cn and hold in back, k1, then p1 from cn.
FC: Sl st to cn and hold in front, p1, then k1 from cn.
T3RP: Sl 2 sts to cn and hold in back, k1, then p1, k1

from cn.

ROW 1: P3, BC, k1, FC, p3.
ROW 2: K3, p1, (k1, p1) twice, k3.
ROW 3: P2, BC, k1, p1, k1, FC, p2.
ROW 4: K2, p1, (k1, p1) 3 times, k2.
ROW 5: P1, BC, k1, (p1, k1) twice, FC, p1.
ROW 6: K1, (p1, k1) 5 times.
ROW 7: BC, k1, (p1, k1) 3 times, FC.
ROW 8: P1, (k1, p1) 5 times.
ROW 9: FC, p1, (k1, p1) 3 times, BC.
ROWS 10, 12, AND 14: Repeat Rows 6, 4, and 2.
ROW 11: P1, FC, p1, (k1, p1) twice, BC, p1.
ROW 13: P2, FC, p1, k1, p1, BC, p2.
ROW 15: P3, FC, p1, BC, p3.
ROW 16: K4, p1, k1, p1, k4.
ROW 17: P4, T3RP, p4.
ROW 18: Repeat Row 16.

Variation: *Double Moss-Stitch Diamonds* (panel of 16 stitches)
This is a widely circulated variation of the moss-stitch diamond. One can only infer that the double in its name refers to its heavier border, because the filling is plain moss stitch.

C6B: Sl 3 sts to cn and hold in back, k3, k3 from cn.
C4R: Sl 1 st to cn and hold in back, k3, k1 from cn.
T4L: Sl 3 sts to cn and hold in front, p1, k3 from cn.
T4R: Sl 1 st to cn and hold in back, k3, p1 from cn.

ROW 1: P4, C4R, T4L, p4.

ROW 2: K4, p3, k1, p4, k4.

ROW 3: P3, C4R, p1, k1, T4L, p3.

ROW 4: K3, p3, k1, p1, k1, p4, k3.

ROW 5: P2, C4R, (p1, k1) twice, T4L, p2.

ROW 6: K2, p3, k1, (p1, k1) twice, p4, k2.

ROW 7: P1, C4R, (p1, k1) 3 times, T4L, p1.

ROW 8: K1, p3, k1, (p1, k1) 3 times, p4, k1.

ROW 9: C4R, (p1, k1) 4 times, T4L.

ROW 10: P3, k1, (p1, k1) 4 times, p4.

ROW 11: T4L, (k1, p1) 4 times, T4R.

ROWS 12, 14, 16, AND 18: Repeat Rows 8, 6, 4, and 2.

ROW 13: P1, T4L, (k1, p1) 3 times, T4R, p1.

ROW 15: P2, T4L, (k1, p1) twice, T4R, p2.

ROW 17: P3, T4L, k1, p1, T4R, p3.

ROW 19: P4, T4L, T4R, p4.

ROW 20: K5, p6, k5.

ROW 21: P5, C6B, p5.

ROW 22: K5, p6, k5.

68a–b.

CUPPED CABLE

Other Name: Branched cable.

General Description: A cupped cable forms a stack of concave-bottomed shapes. This pattern presents the most basic version, simply two lines traveling upward and out to form a cuplike shape with a cable crossing to close the bottom.

In some versions, these cups are worked over more rows so that the cups do not nest inside one another.

Properties:
This pattern forms a textured fabric, but because its broken cables fade into the background of reverse stockinette, the fabric is not as structured as those formed by most cable patterns.

Yarn Consumption:
The twisting draws in the fabric, increasing yarn consumption noticeably.

Suggested Uses:
2–10
The broken cables resemble the stitching up the side of leather chaps, such as those worn by cowboys or rock stars. For a similar effect, try cupped cables up the side of sweater sleeves or knit lounge pants.

Patterns:
FKC: Sl 2 sts to cn and hold in front, k2, then k2 from cn.

BKC: Sl 2 sts to cn and hold in back, k2, then k2 from cn.

SFC: Sl 2 sts to cn and hold in front, p1, then k2 from cn.

SBC: Sl 1 st to cn and hold in back, k2, then p1 from cn.

SFKC: Sl 2 sts to cn and hold in front, k1, then k2 from cn.

SBKC: Sl 1 st to cn and hold in back, k2, then k1 from cn.

Cupped Cable R (panel of 12 stitches)

ROW 1: P3, SBKC, SFKC, p3.
ROW 2: K3, p6, k3.
ROW 3: P2, SBKC, k2, SFKC, p2.
ROW 4: K2, p8, k2.
ROW 5: P1, SBC, k4, SFC, p1.
ROW 6: K1, p2, k1, p4, k1, p2, k1.
ROW 7: SBC, p1, BKC, p1, SFC.
ROW 8: P2, k2, p4, k2, p2.

Cupped Cable L (panel of 12 stitches)

ROW 1: P3, SBKC, SFKC, p3.
ROW 2: K3, p6, k3.
ROW 3: P2, SBKC, k2, SFKC, p2.
ROW 4: K2, p8, k2.
ROW 5: P1, SBC, k4, SFC, p1.
ROW 6: K1, p2, k1, p4, k1, p2, k1.
ROW 7: SBC, p1, FKC, p1, SFC.
ROW 8: P2, k2, p4, k2, p2.

69. **MOSS CUPPED CABLE**

General
Description:

Like goblets filled with wine, these stacked cups are
filled with moss-stitch ripples. An Aran-style panel, its

thick borders are akin to the highly embossed cables for which the Aran sweater is famous.

Properties:

Unlike the plain cupped cable, the bottom of each cup does not sit within the bowl of the cup below it—only one cup is formed over a pattern repeat. The traveling lines create a thick border, and moss-stitch filling adds structure to the fabric while reducing its drape.

Yarn Consumption:

The twisted stitches draw in the fabric, increasing yarn consumption noticeably.

Suggested Uses:

2–8

The border is similar to that of double moss-stitch diamonds. Try combining moss cupped cables with a few simple cables and perhaps the open five-strand braid to make a striking panel for an Aran sweater.

Pattern:

(panel of 15 stitches)

BC: Sl 1 st to cn and hold in back, k2, then p1 from cn.

FC: Sl 2 sts to cn and hold in front, p1, then k2 from cn.

T5L: Sl 2 sts to cn and hold in front, k2, p1, then k2 from cn.

ROW 1: P5, T5L, p5.
ROW 2: K5, p2, k1, p2, k5.
ROW 3: P4, BC, k1, FC, p4.

ROW 4: K4, p2, k1, p1, k1, p2, k4.
ROW 5: P3, BC, k1, p1, k1, FC, p3.
ROW 6: K3, p2, (k1, p1) twice, k1, p2, k3.
ROW 7: P2, BC, (k1, p1) twice, k1, FC, p1.
ROW 8: K2, p2, (k1, p1) 3 times, k1, p2, k2.
ROW 9: P1, BC, (k1, p1) 3 times, k1, FC, p1.
ROW 10: K1, p2, (k1, p1) 4 times, k1, p2, k1.
ROW 11: BC, (k1, p1) 4 times, k1, FC.
ROW 12: P2, (k1, p1) 5 times, k1, p2.

70. 📷   **CUPPED HEART CABLE**

Other Name: Valentine cable.

General Description: Heart-shaped cables are stacked vertically. This pattern avoids the logistical problems associated with forming round traveling-line tops by cleverly splitting the traveling line into two twisted-stitch lines.

Properties: Like most traveling-line cable patterns, this one creates a nonreversible embossed fabric with reduced drape.

Yarn Consumption: The traveling lines and cables draw in the fabric, increasing yarn consumption noticeably.

🧵🧵🧵🧵

Suggested Uses: Flanking a center panel of this pattern with other less-elaborate cables would make a very sweet scarf. To keep the heart design facing right-side up, knit the

2–8

scarf in two pieces, each half the length of the scarf, and then join them in the middle.

Pattern: **(panel of 16 stitches)**

BC: Sl 1 st to cn and hold in back, k2, then p1 from cn.

FC: Sl 2 sts to cn and hold in front, p1, then k2 from cn.

SBC: Sl 1 st to cn and hold in back, k1, then p1 from cn.

SFC: Sl 1 st to cn and hold in front, p1, then k1 from cn.

NOTE: Rows 1–3 are preparatory—repeat only Rows 4–19.

ROWS 1 AND 3: K6, p4, k6.

ROW 2: P6, sl 2 sts to cn and hold in front, k2, then k2 from cn; p6.

ROW 4: P5, BC, FC, p5.

ROW 5: K5, p2, k2, p2, k5.

ROW 6: P4, BC, p2, FC, p4.

ROW 7: (K4, p2) twice, k4.

ROW 8: P3, BC, p4, FC, p3.

ROW 9: K3, p2, k6, p2, k3.

ROW 10: P2, BC twice, FC twice, p2.

ROW 11: K2, (p2, k1, p2, k2) twice.

ROW 12: P1, BC twice, p2, FC twice, p1.

ROW 13: (K1, p2) twice, k4, (p2, k1) twice.

ROW 14: P1, k1, SFC, FC, p2, BC, SBC, k1, p1.

ROW 15: (K1, p1) twice, k1, p2, k2, p2, k1, (p1, k1) twice.

Color Plates

Icon Key

photograph	mindless knitting	requires attention
yarn muffin	needle sizes	stretch
showcases variegated yarns	reversible	

1. **garter stitch**

2a. **stockinette stitch**

2b. **reverse stockinette**

3. **seed stitch**

4. **moss stitch**

5. **double seed stitch**

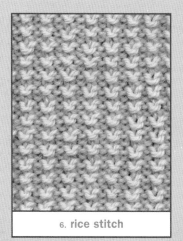

6. **rice stitch**

7a. **dot stitch**

7b. **sand stitch**

8a. **simple diamonds**

8b. **king charles brocade**

8c. **seed stitch diamonds**

8d. **inverness diamonds**

9a. **plain check stitch**

9b. **garter stitch check**

9c. **seed stitch check**

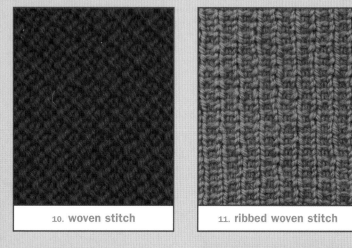

10. **woven stitch**

11. **ribbed woven stitch**

12. **basketweave**

13. **ribbed basketweave**

14. simple chevron

15. deep chevron

16. fancy chevron

17. waving flames

18. **pavilion pattern**

19. **pennant stitch**

20. **pyramid pattern**

21. **parallelograms**

22. **tumbling blocks**

23a. **ladder stitch**

23b. **jacob's ladder**

24a. **lightning stitch**

24b. **heavier lightning stitch**

24c. **double lightning**

25. **horizontal zigzag**

26. **sloped ladders**

27a. **tree motif**

27b. **flag motif**

27c. **anchor motif**

27d. **ship motif**

28. **brioche stitch**

29. **linen stitch**

30. **slip-stitch honeycomb**

31. **slip-stitch trellis**

32. **wildflower knot**

33a. **bricklayer's stitch**

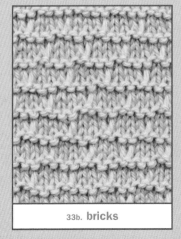

33b. **bricks**

34. **bow ties**

35a. **classic mock cable**

35b. **tamerna stitch**

36. **herringbone**

37a. **plain bobble**

37b. large bobble

37c. blackberry stitch

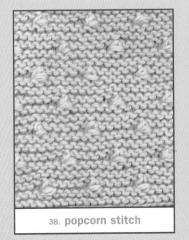

38. popcorn stitch

39a. tiny cable I

39b. **tiny cable r**

39c. **regular cable l**

39d. **regular cable r**

39e. **large cable l**

39f. **large cable r**

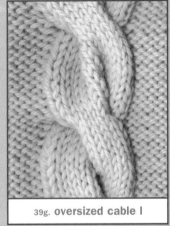

39g. **oversized cable l**

39h. **oversized cable r**

40a. **wave cable l**

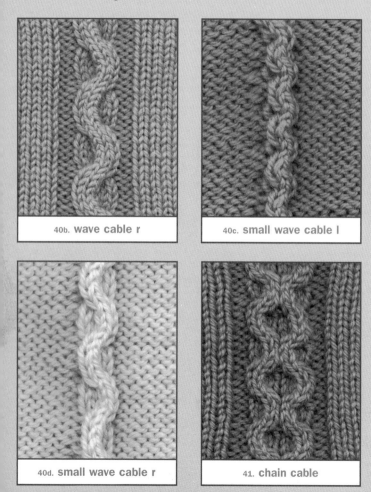

40b. wave cable r

40c. small wave cable l

40d. small wave cable r

41. chain cable

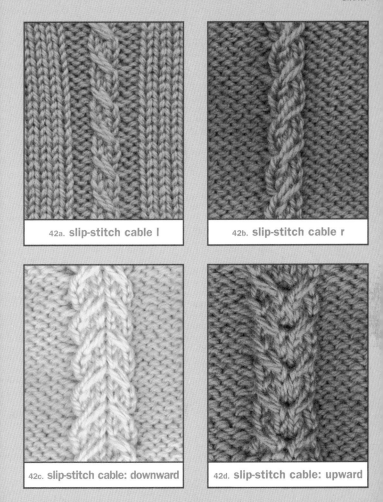

42a. slip-stitch cable l

42b. slip-stitch cable r

42c. slip-stitch cable: downward

42d. slip-stitch cable: upward

43a. **double cable: horseshoe**

43b. **reverse double cable: fishtail**

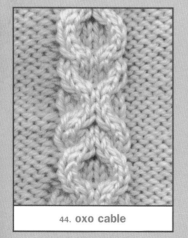

44. **oxo cable**

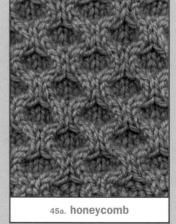

45a. **honeycomb**

45b. **tiny honeycomb**

46a. **staghorn cable**

46b. **reverse staghorn cable**

46c. **small staghorn cable**

46d. reverse small
staghorn cable

47a. small syncopated cable

47b. reverse small
syncopated cable

48a. open syncopated cable

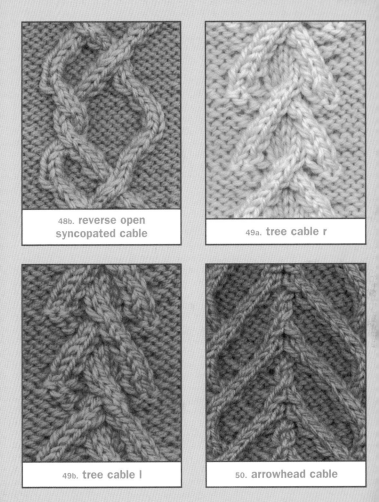

48b. **reverse open syncopated cable**

49a. **tree cable r**

49b. **tree cable l**

50. **arrowhead cable**

51a. **three-strand braid l**

51b. **three-strand braid r**

51c. **reverse three-strand braid**

52a. **four-strand braid**

52b. **five-strand aran braid**

53. **five-strand braid**

54. **open three-strand braid**

55. **open four-strand braid**

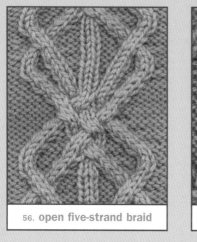

56. **open five-strand braid**

57a. **twisted-stitch waves**

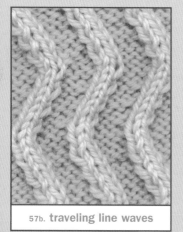

57b. **traveling line waves**

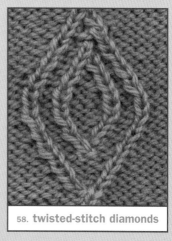

58. **twisted-stitch diamonds**

59a. **twisted-stitch lattice**

59b. **aran lattice**

60. **traveling line whorl**

61. **traveling line double helix**

62a. **ribbed cable l**

62b. **ribble cable r**

63. **waving branches**

64a. **simple split cable**

64b. **interlocking lattice**

65a. **garter stitch cable r**

65b. **garter stitch cable l**

66a. **moss-stitch lattice**

66b. double moss-stitch lattice

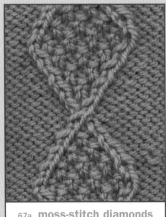

67a. moss-stitch diamonds

67b. double moss-stitch diamonds

68a. cupped cable r

68b. cupped cable I

69. moss cupped cable

70. cupped heart cable

71. moss cupped hearts

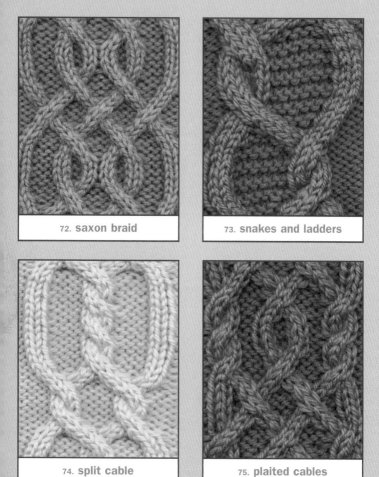

72. **saxon braid**

73. **snakes and ladders**

74. **split cable**

75. **plaited cables**

76. **serpentine cable**

77. **plaid lattice**

78. **smocking stitch**

79. **basket cable**

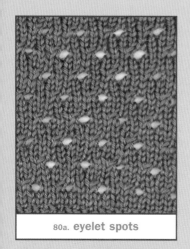

80a. **eyelet spots**

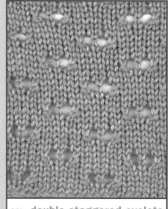

80b. **double staggered eyelets**

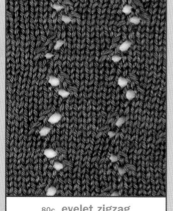

80c. **eyelet zigzag**

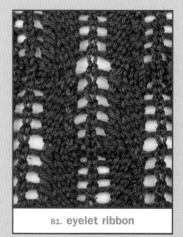

81. **eyelet ribbon**

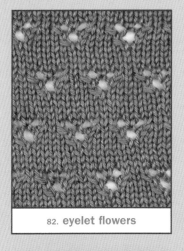

82. eyelet flowers

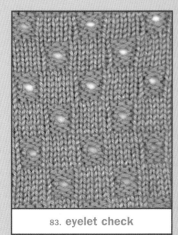

83. eyelet check

84a. eyelet diamonds

84b. simple eyelet diamonds

85. **centered eyelet diamonds**

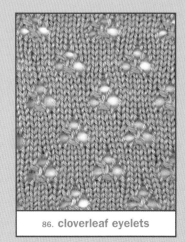

86. **cloverleaf eyelets**

87. **eiffel tower eyelets**

88. **daisy eyelets**

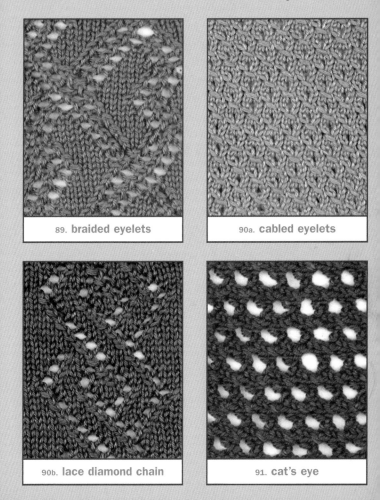

89. **braided eyelets**

90a. **cabled eyelets**

90b. **lace diamond chain**

91. **cat's eye**

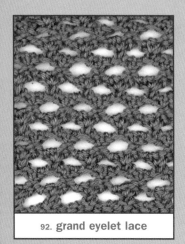

92. grand eyelet lace

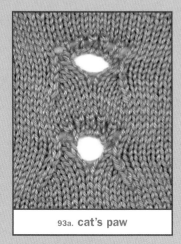

93a. cat's paw

93b. traditional cat's paw

94. faggot check

95. **faggoted zigzag**

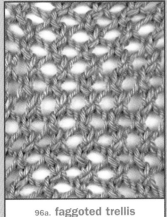

96a. **faggoted trellis**

96b. **lace trellis I**

96c. **faggoted trellis zigzag**

97a. **herringbone faggot**

97b. **herringbone lace**

98. **double herringbone faggot**

99. **purse stitch**

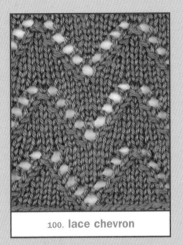

100. **lace chevron**

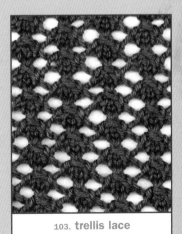

101. **lace feather**

102. **horseshoes**

103. **trellis lace**

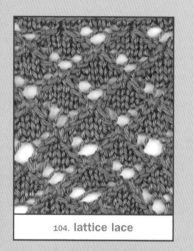

104. **lattice lace**

105a. **lace scales**

105b. **fish-scale lace**

106. **falling leaves**

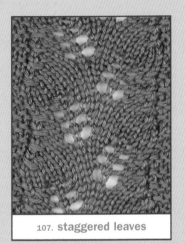

107. **staggered leaves**

108. **flickering flames**

109. **candle flames**

110. **beech leaf**

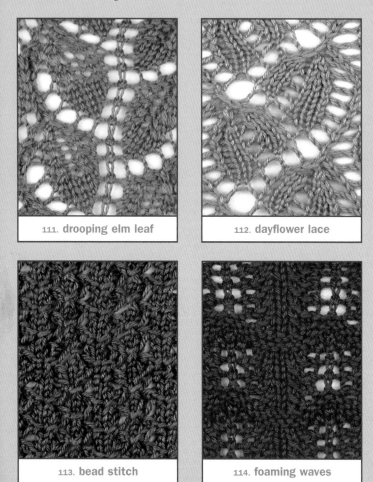

111. **drooping elm leaf**

112. **dayflower lace**

113. **bead stitch**

114. **foaming waves**

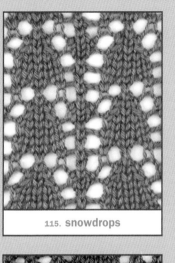

115. snowdrops

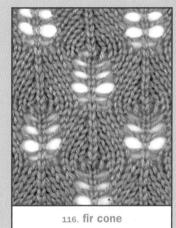

116. fir cone

117. swinging triangles

118. feather and fan

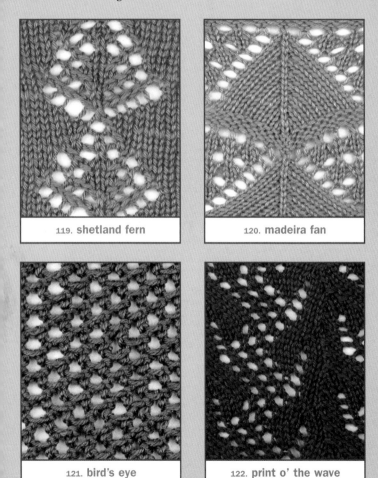

119. **shetland fern**

120. **madeira fan**

121. **bird's eye**

122. **print o' the wave**

123. **obstacles**

124. **catherine wheels**

125. **rose leaf lace**

126. **apple leaf lace**

127. **flemish diamonds**

128a. **arrowhead lace**

128b. **little arrowhead lace**

129. **candelabra panel**

130. **harebell lace**

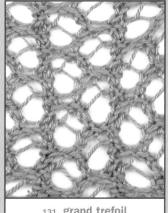

131. **grand trefoil**

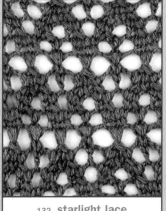

132. **starlight lace**

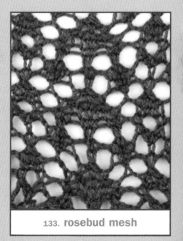

133. **rosebud mesh**

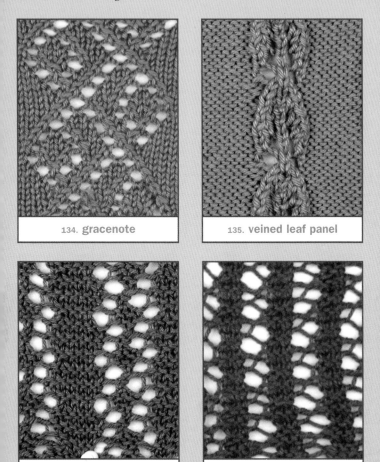

134. **gracenote**

135. **veined leaf panel**

136a. **strawberry**

136b. **fish eye**

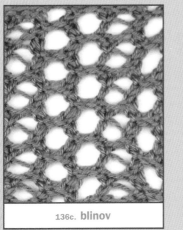

136c. **blinov**

136d. **mouseprint**

137a. **2x2 ribbing**

137b. **1x1 ribbing**

137c. **3x3 ribbing**

137d. **4x2 ribbing**

137e. **5x1 ribbing**

138a. **diagonal ribbing r**

138b. **diagonal ribbing I**

139a. **broken rib**

139b. **stairstep rib**

140. **embossed moss stitch rib**

141. **mistake rib**

142. **fisherman's rib**

143. **slip-stitch ribbing**

144. **faggoting rib**

145a. **cable ribbing l**

145b. **cable ribbing r**

145c. **cable and eyelet ribbing l**

145d. **cable and eyelet ribbing r**

146. **plain hem**

147a. **picot cast-on**

147b. **picot bind-off**

147c. **picot hem**

148a. **single pleat l**

148b. **single pleat r**

148c. **box pleat**

148d. **inverted box pleat**

149a. **kick pleat**

149b. **reverse kick pleat**

150a. **ruffle cast-on**

150b. **ruffle cast-on plus**

150c. **basic ruffle bind-off**

150d. **layered basic ruffle**

151a. **small bell ruffle cast-on**

151b. **small bell ruffle bind-off**

152a. **large bell ruffle cast-on**

152b. **large bell ruffle bind-off**

153. **point edging**

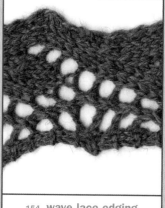

154. **wave lace edging**

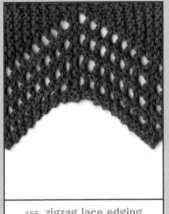

155. **zigzag lace edging**

156. **leaf edging**

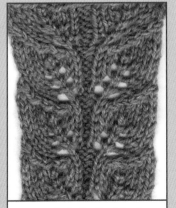

157. **twin leaf edging**

158. **narrow van dyke**

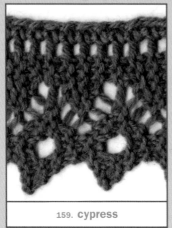

159. **cypress**

160. **aran braid with fringe**

161a. **i-cord edging**

161b. **eyelet cord edging**

ROW 16: P1, k1, p1, SFC, FC, BC, SBC, p1, k1, p1.

ROW 17: K1, p1, k2, p1, k1, p4, k1, p1, k2, p1, k1.

ROW 18: P1, SFC, SBC, p1, sl 2 sts to cn and hold in front, k2, then k2 from cn; p1, SFC, SBC, p1.

ROW 19: K2, sl 1 st to cn and hold in back, k1, then k1 from cn; k2, p4, k2, sl 1 st to cn and hold in front, k1, then k1 from cn; k2.

---

71. **MOSS CUPPED HEARTS**

Other Names: Moss-stitch hearts.

General Description: This fancy Aran-style panel fills curving twisted-stitch lines with moss stitch and a pearl-drop center. The number of stitches within the panel varies from row to row; inconsistency does not necessarily indicate a dropped stitch or an accidental increase.

Properties: The textured fabric remains relatively flat except for the large, pearl-shaped cable in the center of each heart. The moss-stitch filling helps keep this pattern evenly tensioned.

Yarn Consumption: The traveling lines and pearl cable draw in the fabric, increasing yarn consumption noticeably.

Suggested Uses: This pattern would be an elaborate addition to any
\ 2–8   project. Consider using it for a festive holiday sweater
                  or as a panel in a delicate cashmere scarf.

Pattern: **(panel of 15 stitches)**

> **T2B:** Sl 1 st to cn and hold in back, k1, then p1 from
> cn.
> **T2F:** Sl 1 st to cn and hold in front, p1, then k1 from
> cn.
> **C2B:** Sl 1 st to cn and hold in back, k1, then k1 from
> cn.
> **C2F:** Sl 1 st to cn and hold in front, k1, then k1 from
> cn.
>
> **ROW 1:** P3, T2B, (k1, p1) twice, k1, T2F, p3.
> **ROW 2:** K3, p2, (k1, p1) twice, k1, p2, k3.
> **ROW 3:** P2, C2B, (p1, k1) 3 times, p1, C2F, p2.
> **ROW 4:** K2, (p1, k1) 5 times, p1, k2.
> **ROW 5:** P1, T2B, (k1, p1) twice, M3, (p1, k1) twice,
> T2F, p1. (17 sts)
> **ROW 6:** K1, p2, k1, p1, k1, p5, k1, p1, k1, p2, k1.
> **ROW 7:** C2B, (p1, k1) twice, p1, M1, k3, M1, (p1,
> k1) twice, p1, C2F.
> **ROW 8:** (P1, k1) 3 times, p7, (k1, p1) 3 times.
> **ROW 9:** KB1, (k1, p1) 3 times, M1, k5, M1, (p1, k1)
> 3 times, KB1.
> **ROW 10:** (P1, k1) 3 times, p9, (k1, p1) 3 times.
> **ROW 11:** KB1, (k1, p1) 3 times, k2, sl 1, k2tog, psso,

k2, (p1, k1) 3 times, KB1. (19 sts)

ROW 12: Repeat Row 8.

ROW 13: KB1, (k1, p1) 3 times, k1, sl 1, k2tog, psso, k1, (p1, k1) 3 times, KB1. (17 sts)

ROW 14: (P1, k1) 3 times, p5, (k1, p1) 3 times.

ROW 15: KB1, (k1, p1) 3 times, yb, sl 1, k2tog, psso, (p1, k1) 3 times, KB1. (15 sts)

ROW 16: (P1, k1) 3 times, p3, (k1, p1) 3 times.

ROW 17: T2F, p1, k1, p1, T2B, k1, T2F, p1, k1, p1, T2B.

ROW 18: K1, p2, (k1, p3) twice, k1, p2, k1.

ROW 19: P1, T2F, k1, C2B, p1, k1, p1, C2F, k1, T2B, p1.

ROW 20: K4, (p1, k1) 3 times, p1, k4.

---

72. 📷 **SAXON BRAID**

Other Name: Six-strand cable.

General
Description: This intricate braid with its curved sides is reminiscent of a Celtic knot, though a braid's bands will travel on as long as one is willing to repeat the panel pattern. A Celtic knot's bands, however, turn back on themselves to form a closed loop, giving the pattern a definite beginning and end.

Properties: The multiple cable crossings create a thicker fabric with reduced drape, which is slightly mitigated by the purl stitches separating each band. Despite an intricate appearance, this pattern is not difficult to work, particularly once the braid begins to take shape.

Yarn Consumption:

The multiple cable crossings and traveling lines draw in the fabric, increasing yarn consumption substantially.

Suggested Uses:

Saxon braid would make a stunning center panel down the front of a tunic or sweater. Its overt Celtic or Norse patterning would be at home in any project with a related theme.

Pattern:

(panel of 24 stitches)

BC: Sl 2 sts to cn and hold in back, k2, then p2 from cn.

BKC: Sl 2 sts to cn and hold in back, k2, then k2 from cn.

FC: Sl 2 sts to cn and hold in front, p2, then k2 from cn.

FKC: Sl 2 sts to cn and hold in front, k2, then k2 from cn.

SBC: Sl 1 st to cn and hold in back, k2, then p1 from cn.

SFC: Sl 2 sts to cn and hold in front, p1, then k2 from cn.

ROW 1: P2, BKC, (p4, BKC) twice, p2.
ROW 2: K2, p4, (k4, p4) twice, k2.
ROW 3: P1, SBC, (FC, BC) twice, SFC, p1.

ROW 4: K1, p2, k3, p4, k4, p4, k3, p2, k1.
ROW 5: SBC, p3, FKC, p4, FKC, p3, SFC.
ROW 6: P2, k4, (p4, k4) twice, p2.
ROW 7: K2, p3, SBC, FC, BC, SFC, p3, k2.
ROW 8: (P2, k3) twice, p4, (k3, p2) twice.
ROW 9: (K2, p3) twice, k4, (p3, k2) twice.
ROWS 10, 12, AND 14: Repeat Rows 8, 6, and 4.
ROW 11: K2, p3, SFC, BC, FC, SBC, p3, k2.
ROW 13: SFC, p3, FKC, p4, FKC, p3, SBC.
ROW 15: P1, SFC, (BC, FC) twice, SBC, p1.
ROW 16: Repeat Row 2.

---

73. **SNAKES AND LADDERS**

General
Description:

This simple pattern has a very clever appearance—as its name implies, slithering cables wind around a garter-stitch ladder. The cables are based on a basic split or syncopated pattern, and its filling makes the pattern jump from its background of reverse stockinette.

Properties:

The lateral stretch of the garter stitch filling partially mitigates the lateral pull of the cable pattern, creating an even-tensioned, embossed fabric with both horizontal and vertical stretch.

Yarn
Consumption:

The cable crossings and traveling lines eat up yarn, increasing yarn consumption.

Suggested Uses: This pattern sways back and forth like a falling ribbon.
  2–8 Use it at a fine gauge to add delicate yet interesting
    curves in a woman's sweater or at a heavier gauge to
    add a fun, geometric swirl in a child's sweater.

Pattern: **(panel of 19 stitches)**

> **T4L:** Sl 3 sts to cn and hold in front, p1, then k3
>   from cn.
> **T4R:** Sl 1 st to cn and hold in back, k3, then p1 from
>   cn.
> **C4L:** Sl 3 sts to cn and hold in front, k1, then k3
>   from cn.
> **C4R:** Sl 1 st to cn and hold in back, k3, then k1 from
>   cn.
> **C6F:** Sl 3 sts to cn and hold in front, k3, then k3
>   from cn.
> **C6B:** Sl 1 st to cn and hold in back, k3, then k3 from
>   cn.
> **CR5BR:** Sl 2 sts to cn and hold in back, k3, then k2
>   from cn.
> **CR5FL:** Sl 3 sts to cn and hold in front, k2, then k3
>   from cn.
>
> **ROW 1 (WS):** K3, p6, k6, p3, k1.
> **ROW 2:** P1, T4L, k3, Cr5BR, C4L, p2.
> **ROW 3:** K2, p3, (k3, p3) twice, k2.
> **ROW 4:** P2, T4L, Cr5BR, k3, C4L, p1.
> **ROW 5:** K1, p3, k6, p6, k3.

ROW 6: P3, C6B, k6, C4L.

ROW 7: P3, k7, p6, k3.

ROW 8: P3, k16.

ROWS 9–13: (Repeat Rows 7 and 8) twice, then repeat Row 7 again.

ROW 14: P3, C6B, k6, T4R.

ROW 15: Repeat Row 5.

ROW 16: P2, C4R, Cr5FL, k3, T4R, p1.

ROW 17: Repeat Row 3.

ROW 18: P1, C4R, k3, Cr5FL, T4R, p2.

ROW 19: Repeat Row 1.

ROW 20: C4R, k6, C6F, p3.

ROW 21: K3, p6, k7, p3.

ROW 22: K16, p3.

ROWS 23–27: (Repeat Rows 21 and 22) twice, then repeat Row 21 again.

ROW 28: T4L, k6, C6F, p3.

74. **SPLIT CABLE**

General Description:

In this Aran-style cable, two pairs of traveling lines cross in a simple cable and then split from their partners to cross with a line from the other pair, creating a fancy, ropelike pattern.

Properties:
↔

This pattern creates a thick, structured fabric with limited drape and moderate lateral stretch.

Yarn
Consumption:

Suggested Uses:
2–10

Pattern:

The multiple crossings draw in the fabric, increasing yarn consumption substantially.

A good choice as a central panel on a thick winter sweater, this pattern could be extended around a V-neck by diverting one cable to each side of the collar.

(panel of 16 stitches)

BC: Sl 2 sts to cn and hold in back, k2, then p2 from cn.
FC: Sl 2 sts to cn and hold in front, p2, then k2 from cn.
FKC: Sl 2 sts to cn and hold in front, k2, then k2 from cn.

ROW 1: P2, FKC, p4, FKC, p2.
ROW 2 AND ALL SUBSEQUENT WRONG-SIDE ROWS: Knit all knit sts and purl all purl sts.
ROW 3: P2, k4, p4, k4, p2.
ROW 5: Repeat Row 1.
ROW 7: (BC, FC) twice.
ROW 9: K2, p4, FKC, p4, k2.
ROW 11: K2, p4, k4, p4, k2.
ROWS 13–22: (Repeat Rows 9–12) twice, then repeat Rows 9 and 10.
ROW 23: (FC, BC) twice.
ROW 24: Repeat Row 2.

75. **PLAITED CABLES**

General
Description:

A split cable pattern, this pattern forms a dense field of swirling cables, resembling intricate iron grillwork. The pattern alternates between double crossings and triple crossings, which break up the crowded field of traveling bands nicely.

Properties:

↔

This pattern creates a thick, embossed fabric with reduced drape. Its allover cabling gives the fabric a fair amount of lateral stretch, though it is too heavy to hug curves like some simple ribbings do.

Yarn
Consumption:

Suggested Uses:

╲ 2–10

The dense traveling lines and bountiful cable crossings draw in the fabric significantly and devour yarn.

Plaited cables would make an impressive center panel for any Aran-style sweater. Consider flanking it with filled cables or any solid pattern to anchor the complex twirling of the plaited cables.

Pattern:

(16 stitch + 8 repeat)

FC: Sl 2 sts to cn and hold in front, p2, then k2 from cn.
BC: Sl 2 sts to cn and hold in back, k2, then p2 from cn.
FKC: Sl 2 sts to cn and hold in front, k2, then k2 from cn.

BKC: Sl 2 sts to cn and hold in back, k2, then k2 from cn.

ROW 1: P2, BKC, * p4, BKC; rep from * to last 2 sts, p2.

ROW 2: K4, p4, * k4, p4; rep from * to last 2 sts, k2.

ROW 3: P2, k2, * FC, BC; rep from * to last 4 sts, k2, p2.

ROW 4: K2, p2, k2, p4, * k4, p4; rep from * to last 6 sts, k2, p2, k2.

ROW 5: P2, k2, p2, FKC, * p4, FKC; rep from * to last 6 sts, p2, k2, p2.

ROW 6: Repeat Row 4.

ROW 7: P2, k2, * p2, BC, FC; rep from * to last 4 sts, k2, p2.

ROW 8: Repeat Row 2.

ROWS 9 AND 10: Repeat Rows 1 and 2.

ROW 11: P2, k4, * p2, BC, FC, p2, k4; rep from * to last 2 sts, p2.

ROW 12: K2, p4, k2, * p2, k4, p2, k2, p4, k2; rep from * to end.

ROW 13: P2, BKC, p2, * k2, p4, k2, p2, BKC, p2; rep from * to end.

ROW 14: Repeat Row 12.

ROW 15: P2, k4, p2, * FC, BC, p2, k4, p2; rep from * to end.

ROW 16: Repeat Row 2.

76. 📷 **SERPENTINE CABLE**

General
Description:

A larger, simpler version of the plaited cables pattern, these intertwining cables are all double crossings.

Properties:
↻↔

The allover cabling creates a dense, embossed fabric, and the offsetting rows alternate between right and left crosses to give this pattern a balanced feel. When designing a project, note that the pattern needs to be worked over a minimum of 20 stitches to show the full pattern.

Yarn
Consumption:

🧵🧵🧵🧵🧵

The multiple cable crossings and traveling lines draw in the fabric and increase yarn consumption substantially.

Suggested Uses:
╲ 2–10

Like any Aran-style cable panel, serpentine cables are well suited to the center of a sweater. The balanced crossings lend this pattern a feeling of length, so try it on a rectangular shoulder bag with a long vertical edge, such as beaded macramé bags just the right size for a book, sock knitting, and a wallet. For extra fun, add tassels off the bottom seam.

Pattern:

FC: Sl 2 sts to cn and hold in front, p1, then k2 from cn.

BC: Sl 1 st to cn and hold in back, k2, then p1 from cn.

FKC: Sl 2 sts to cn and hold in front, k2, then k2 from cn.

BKC: Sl 2 sts to cn and hold in back, k2, then k2 from cn.

(multiple of 8 stitches + 4)

ROW 1 (WS): K2, p2, * k4, p4; rep from *, end last repeat k4, p2, k2.

ROW 2: P2, * FC, p2, BC; rep from *, end p2.

ROW 3 AND ALL SUBSEQUENT WRONG-SIDE ROWS: Knit all knit sts and purl all purl sts.

ROW 4: P3, * FC, BC, p2; rep from *, end p1.

ROW 6: * P4, BKC; rep from *, end p4.

ROW 8: P3, * BC, FC, p2; rep from *, end p1.

ROW 10: Knit all knit sts and purl all purl sts.

ROW 12: P3, * FC, BC, p2; rep from *, end p1.

ROW 14: Repeat Row 6.

ROW 16: P3, * BC, FC, p2; rep from *, end p1.

ROW 18: P2, * BC, p2, FC; rep from *, end p2.

ROW 20: P1, BC, * p4, FKC; rep from *, end last repeat p4, FC, p1.

ROW 22: BC, p4, * BC, FC, p2; rep from *, end last repeat p2, FC.

ROW 24: Knit all knit sts and purl all purl sts.

ROW 26: FC, p4, * FC, BC, p2; rep from *, end last repeat p2, BC.

ROW 28: P1, FC, * p4, FKC; rep from *, end last repeat p4, BC, p1.

77. 📷 **PLAID LATTICE**

Other Names: X-in-a-diamond, trellis diamond.

General Description: This pattern, complete with thick diamonds and intercrossing lines of twisted stitches, is as close as an embossed cable pattern gets to mimicking traditional Scottish argyle. Argyle purists, however, would insist that true argyle is made only from specific colorwork patterns and scoff at this liberal use of the term.

Properties: The combination of traveling lines and twist-stitch lines crisscrossing throughout the pattern creates a thick, layered fabric with minimal drape.

Yarn Consumption: The multiple crossings and twist-stitch patterning draw in the fabric, increasing yarn consumption significantly.

Suggested Uses: Tweak the argyle purists by using plaid lattice in a mock-argyle sweater vest or knitting mock-argyle knee socks on smaller needles. For a nontweaking alternative, make the sweater and socks, but name them with the proper title of the stitch. For a non-garment alternative, this pattern would make a handsome and comfortable cushion for a chair or a footstool.

Pattern: **(multiple of 14 stitches + 2)**

BC: Sl 1 st to cn and hold in back, k2, then p1 from cn.

BKC: Sl 1 st to cn and hold in back, k2, then k1 tbl from cn.

FC: Sl 2 sts to cn and hold in front, p1, then k2 from cn.

FKC: Sl 2 st to cn and hold in front, k1 tbl, then k2 from cn.

SBC: Sl 1 st to cn and hold in back, k1 tbl, then p1 from cn.

SFC: Sl 1 st to cn and hold in front, p1, then k1 tbl from cn.

ROW 1 (WS): K1, * p1, k4, p4, k4, p1; rep from *, end k1.

ROW 2: P1, k1 tbl, * p4, sl 2 sts to cn and hold in front, k2, then k2 from cn; p4, sl 1 st to cn and hold in front, k1 tbl, then k1 tbl from cn; rep from * to last 2 sts, end last repeat k1 tbl, p1.

ROW 3 AND ALL SUBSEQUENT WRONG-SIDE ROWS: Knit all knit sts and purl all purl sts.

ROW 4: P1, * SFC, p2, BC, FC, p2, SBC; rep from *, end p1.

ROW 6: P1, * p1, SFC, BC, p2, FC, SBC, p1; rep from *, end p1.

ROW 8: P1, * p2, BKC, p4, FKC, p2; rep from *, end p1.

ROW 10: P1, * p1, BC, SFC, p2, SBC, FC, p1; rep from *, end p1.

ROW 12: P1, * BC, p2, SFC, SBC, p2, FC, p1; rep from *, end p1.

ROW 14: P1, k2, * p4, sl 1 st to cn and hold in back,

k1 tbl, then k1 tbl from cn; p4, sl 2 sts to cn and hold in back, k2, then k2 from cn; rep from * to last 3 sts, end last repeat k2, p1.

ROW 16: P1, * FC, p2, SBC, SFC, p2, BC; rep from *, end p1.

ROW 18: P1, * p1, FC, SBC, p2, SFC, BC, p1; rep from *, end p1.

ROW 20: P1, * p2, FKC, p4, BKC, p2; rep from *, end p1.

ROW 22: P1, * p1, SBC, FC, p2, BC, SFC, p1; rep from *, end p1.

ROW 24: P1, * SBC, p2, FC, BC, p2, SFC; rep from *, end p1.

---

78. 📷 **SMOCKING STITCH**

General Description:
Smocking wraps yarn around stitches to draw them together like two curtain panels. The standard version presented here binds raised stockinette rows of 2x2 ribbing together, alternating between binding to the right and left to create a lattice pattern.

Properties:
This pattern creates a thick, layered fabric. The smocking wraps stabilize the fabric, reducing its lateral stretch.

Yarn Consumption:
🧵🧵🧵🧵
The ribbing's tendency to draw in the fabric is mitigated by the alternating wraps, causing the yarn consumption to increase noticeably but not substantially.

Suggested Uses:
2–6

Smocking stitch's thickness makes it suitable for heavy winter sweaters, though its use should be avoided in any part of the garment that would incorporate shaping—increases or decreases would spoil the patterning. The cushioned fabric is also ideal for upholstery projects.

Pattern: **(multiple of 8 stitches + 2)**

ROWS 1 AND 3 (WS): K2, * p2, k2; rep from *.
ROW 2: P2, * k2, p2; rep from *.
ROW 4: P2, * insert RH needle from front between 6th and 7th sts on LH needle and draw through a loop; sl this loop onto LH needle and knit it together with the 1st st on LH needle; k1, p2, k2, p2; rep from *.
ROWS 5 AND 7: Repeat Rows 1 and 3.
ROW 6: Repeat Row 2.
ROW 8: P2, k2, p2, * draw loop from between 6th and 7th sts as before and knit it together with 1st st, then k1, p2, k2, p2; rep from *, end k2, p2.

---

79. **BASKET CABLE**

Other Names: Basket panel, basketweave cable.

General Description:
The allover pattern of crossing eight-stitch cables gives fabric made with this pattern depth and the look of tiny interlocking pillows.

Properties:
⟷

This pattern forms a dense, layered fabric with a lofty appearance in contrast to its rather structured feel. Note that this pattern needs to be worked over a minimum of 20 stitches for the pattern to form.

Yarn Consumption:

The allover cables draw in the fabric considerably, causing the pattern to enthusiastically consume yarn.

Suggested Uses:
2–8

Though this pattern is popular in sweaters, its bulky appearance and tendency to stretch and distort may convince a knitter to try it first in a nongarment project, or at least in a garment for which the fit is not particularly important.

Pattern:

(multiple of 8 stitches + 4)

ROWS 1, 3, AND 5 (WS): K2, purl to last 2 sts, k2.
ROWS 2 AND 4: Knit.
ROW 6: K2, * sl 4 sts to cn and hold in back, k4, then k4 from cn; rep from *, end k2.
ROWS 7, 9, AND 11: K2, purl to last 2 sts, k2.
ROW 12: K6, * sl 4 sts to cn and hold in front, k4, then k4 from cn; rep from *, end k6.

Openwork and Lace

80a–c. 📷 **EYELET SPOTS**

Other Name: Staggered eyelets.

General
Description:
Generally, eyelet patterns are a subset of the larger lace world, identified by their small, open spots arranged on an otherwise solid background. These small holes are formed by pairing a yarn-over with a decrease—typically skp/ssk or k2tog—and their basic construction makes working an eyelet pattern a good introduction to lace knitting.

Properties:
The fabric formed by this pattern will be similar to, though slightly more delicate than, stockinette, with good drape and normal elasticity.

Yarn
Consumption:
The eyelets do not open the fabric enough to use much less yarn than stockinette.

Suggested Uses:
The basic pattern is surprisingly effective in giving a garment delicacy and interest. Any version of eyelet spots would be suitable substitutes for stockinette in almost any application.

Pattern:

(multiple of 4 stitches + 3)

ROW 1: Knit.
ROW 2 AND ALL OTHER WRONG-SIDE ROWS: Purl.
ROW 3: * K2, k2tog, yo, rep from * to last 3 sts, k3.
ROW 5: Knit.
ROW 7: * K2tog, yo, k2; rep from * to last 3 sts, k2tog, yo, k1.
ROW 8: Purl.

Variations:

Double Staggered Eyelets or *Allover Eyelets* (multiple of 10 stitches +1)
The double staggered eyelets look like tiny hearts or fireflies and would be a pretty addition to any summer blouse or tank.

ROW 1: Knit.
ROW 2 AND ALL OTHER WRONG-SIDE ROWS: Purl.
ROW 3: K3, * k2tog, yo, k1, yo, skp, k5; rep from * to last 8 sts, k2tog, yo, k1, yo, skp, k3.
ROW 5: Knit.
ROW 7: K1, * yo, skp, k5, k2tog, yo, k1; rep from *.
ROW 8: Purl.

Eyelet Zigzag (multiple of 7 stitches)
These eyelet zigzags are like small climbing vines and would serve nicely as a dainty trim or allover pattern.

ROW 1: * K2, k2tog, yo, k3; rep from *.

ROW 2 AND ALL OTHER WRONG-SIDE ROWS: Purl.

ROW 3: * K1, k2tog, yo, k4; rep from *.

ROW 5: Knit.

ROW 7: K3, yo, skp, k2; rep from *.

ROW 9: K4, yo, skp, k1; rep from *.

ROW 11: Knit.

ROW 12: Purl.

---

81. **EYELET RIBBON**

Other Name: Ribbon rib.

General Description: This lace ribbon is a simple pattern that creates a fascinating fabric—it utilizes the bias of the decreases to give each stockinette band curving lines, like stylized sun rays emanating from yarn-over centers.

Properties: When knit with very fine yarn, the fabric is intriguing: The offsetting tension of each band pulls the thin ladders of yarn-overs like cobwebs. The vertical strips of neighboring yarn-overs give the fabric more drape and elasticity than stockinette.

Yarn Consumption: The double rows of yarn-overs open up the fabric, decreasing yarn consumption noticeably.

Suggested Uses: For a deceptively simple stole, add a simple border to a handful of repeats and knit this pattern until it

00–8

measures the length of your wingspan. Also consider eyelet ribbon for a simple mesh top to be worn over a tank for a punk/goth look.

Pattern: **(multiple of 14 stitches + 1)**

ROW 1 (WS) AND ALL OTHER WRONG-SIDE ROWS: Purl.
ROWS 2, 4, 6, 8, AND 10: K1, * yo, k3, sk2p, yo, k1, yo, k3tog, k3, yo, k1; rep from *.
ROWS 12, 14, 16, 18, AND 20: K1, * yo, k3tog, k3, yo, k1, yo, k3, sk2p, yo, k1; rep from *.

---

82. 📷 **EYELET FLOWERS**

Other Name: Little flowers.

General Description: Another good example of the eyelet genre, this pattern fashions three eyelets into a small V to look like tiny rosebuds.

Properties: The fabric formed by this pattern shares many of the qualities of its base stitch, stockinette, such as good drape and moderate elasticity. However, the open patterning adds an airiness and delicacy not found in solid patterns.

Yarn Consumption: The triple eyelet pattern opens up the fabric and, when worked over a larger area, decreases yarn consumption.

Suggested Uses:

2–8

Eyelet flowers would be a very nice allover pattern for any garment or bag, but also try working the pattern over only the first eight rows to create a single band of flowers as an armband or waist trim on a blouse.

Pattern:

(multiple of 6 stitches + 3)

ROW 1: Knit.
ROW 2 AND ALL OTHER WRONG-SIDE ROWS: Purl.
ROW 3: Knit.
ROW 5: *K4, yo, skp; rep from *, end k3.
ROW 7: K2, k2tog, yo, k1, yo, skp, *k1, k2tog, yo, k1, yo, skp; rep from *, end k2.
ROWS 9 AND 11: Knit.
ROW 13: K1, yo, skp, * k4, yo, skp; rep from *.
ROW 15: K2, yo, skp, k1, k2tog, yo, * k1, yo, skp, k1, k2tog, yo; rep from *, end k2.
ROW 16: Purl.

83.

EYELET CHECK

General Description:

This pattern creates a checkerboard of knit-stitch and purl-stitch blocks, with eyelets centered in each purl-stitch block. The purl-stitch blocks accentuate the long vertical strip of knit stitches bordering each eyelet check, lengthening the fabric and making the eyelet blocks look like little birdhouses nestled in tall trees.

Properties:
↔

The alternating blocks create a broken ribbing, which gives this fabric increased vertical elasticity and a bit more structure than stockinette.

Yarn
Consumption:

Though the eyelets create holes in the fabric, there are not enough of them to decrease yarn usage.

Suggested Uses:
\ 0–8

This pattern is very geometric and would be suited to boxy jackets, modular sweaters, and fun handbags. For an interesting cushion, knit two square panels of equal size, line them with a contrasting fabric, and stuff. The eyelets will act as windows to the fabric beneath, adding depth and visual interest to the project.

Pattern:

(multiple of 8 stitches + 3)

ROW 1: K2, * p3, k5; rep from *, end k1.
ROW 2: P1, * p5, k3; rep from *, end p2.
ROW 3: K2, * p1, yo, p2tog, k5; rep from *, end k1.
ROW 4: P1, * p5, k3; rep from *, end p2.
ROW 5: K2, * p3, k5; rep from *, end k1.
ROW 6: Purl.
ROW 7: K1, * k5, p3; rep from *, end k2.
ROW 8: P2, * k3, p5; rep from *, end p1.
ROW 9: K1, * k5, p1, yo, p2tog; rep from *, end k2.
ROW 10: P2, * k3, p5; rep from *, end p1.
ROW 11: K1, * k5, p3; rep from *, end k2.
ROW 12: Purl.

EYELET DIAMONDS

General
Description:

This pattern creates fairly large, diagonally stacked
eyelet diamonds, with eyelets in the center of each. If
looked at askance, one might mistake the pattern for
stacked snake-eyes dice; if desired, the eyelet in the
center could be easily removed to counter this effect.

Properties:

The fabric formed by this pattern will be similar to,
though slightly more delicate than, stockinette, with
good drape and normal elasticity. The equal pairing of
decreases and increases creates an even tension.

Yarn
Consumption:

The diagonal lines of yarn-overs open up the fabric,
decreasing yarn consumption noticeably.

Suggested Uses:

\ 0–8

Though it would make for a fun bolero or wrap, this
pattern could also serve as a center motif for a more
substantial lace shawl or stole. Consider bordering it
with other eyelet patterns to keep the fabric's density
consistent.

Pattern:

(multiple of 10 stitches + 4)

ROW 1: K2, yo, ssk, * k1, k2tog, (yo) twice, ssk; rep
from * to last 5 sts, k1, k2tog, yo, k2.
ROW 2 AND ALL OTHER WRONG-SIDE ROWS: Purl.
Throughout Rows 2 and 10, purl into the front
and back of every "(yo) twice" of previous row.

ROW 3: K2, * k2tog, yo, k6, yo, ssk; rep from *, end k2.

ROW 5: K3, * k2tog, yo, k4, yo, ssk, k2; rep from *, end k1.

ROW 7: K4, * k2tog, yo, k2, yo, ssk, k4; rep from *.

ROW 9: K2, yo, ssk, * k1, k2tog, (yo) twice, ssk; rep from * to last 5 sts, k1, k2tog, yo, k2.

ROW 11: K5, * yo, ssk, k2tog, yo, k6; rep from *, end last repeat k5.

ROW 13: K4, * yo, ssk, k2, k2tog, yo, k4; rep from *.

ROW 15: K3, * yo, ssk, k4, k2tog, yo, k2; rep from *, end k1.

ROW 16: Purl.

Variation: *Simple Eyelet Diamonds* (multiple of 8 stitches + 7)
Technically a variation of eyelet diamonds, this pattern more closely resembles eyelet flowers in its simple arrangement of four eyelets to create small, staggered diamonds.

ROW 1: Knit.

ROW 2 AND ALL OTHER WRONG-SIDE ROWS: Purl.

ROW 3: K3, * yo, skp, k6; rep from * to last 4 sts, yo, skp, k2.

ROW 5: K2, * yo, sk2p, yo, k5; rep from * to last 5 sts, yo, sk2p, yo, k2.

ROW 7: Repeat Row 3.

ROW 9: Knit.

ROW 11: K7, * yo, skp, k6; rep from *.

ROW 13: K6, * yo, sk2p, yo, k5; rep from * to last st, k1.
ROW 15: Repeat Row 11.
ROW 16: Purl.

85.

CENTERED EYELET DIAMONDS

Other Name: Lozenge lace panel.

General
Description: This pattern forms larger eyelet diamonds on a background of stockinette. As a panel, it does not require creating an allover pattern.

Properties: The fabric is similar to, though slightly more delicate than, stockinette, with good drape and normal elasticity. The equal pairing of decreases and increases creates an even tension.

Yarn
Consumption: Though the eyelets create holes in the fabric, there are not enough of them to decrease yarn usage. If worked repeatedly, close together, over a large area, a small decrease may be noticed.

Suggested Uses: This pattern would make an elegant design down the
\ 0–6 side or center of a sweater. Try knitting it into a skirt and lining the skirt with a bold fabric—if sewing a lining isn't appealing, either end the pattern at an appropriate distance from the waistband or wear a saucy pair of stockings.

Pattern: **(multiple of 11 stitches)**

ROW 1: K1, yo, skp, k5, k2tog, yo, k1.
ROW 2 AND ALL OTHER WRONG-SIDE ROWS: Purl.
ROW 3: K2, yo, skp, k3, k2tog, yo, k2.
ROW 5: K3, yo, skp, k1, k2tog, yo, k3.
ROW 7: K4, yo, sk2p, yo, k4.
ROW 9: K3, k2tog, yo, k1, yo, skp, k3.
ROW 11: K2, k2tog, yo, k3, yo, skp, k2.
ROW 13: K1, k2tog, yo, k5, yo, skp, k1.
ROW 15: K2tog, yo, k7, yo, skp.
ROW 16: Purl.

86. **CLOVERLEAF EYELETS**

General
Description:

A double-decrease offsets the two yarn-overs in Row 4, which creates the base of this delicate eyelet pattern of upside-down Vs. The double-decrease thickens the fabric slightly and anchors the pattern in its sea of stockinette.

Properties:

The fabric formed by this pattern will be similar to, though slightly more delicate than, stockinette, with good drape and normal elasticity. The double-decrease in the center of each clover gives the fabric a subtle texture, as well.

Yarn
Consumption:

Worked over a large area, the allover eyelet patterning opens up the fabric and decreases yarn consumption.

Suggested Uses:
\ 0–6

The delicate pattern makes cloverleaf eyelets an obvious candidate for pretty summer sweaters and easy baby blankets. However, its meshlike qualities make it suitable for a throwback to the 1980s, when mesh tops were all the rage. Knit something with off-the-shoulder shaping for a particularly authentic look.

Pattern:

(multiple of 8 stitches + 7)

ROW 1 (WS) AND ALL OTHER WRONG-SIDE ROWS: Purl.

ROW 2: Knit.

ROW 4: K2, yo, sk2p, yo, * k5, yo, sk2p, yo; rep from *, end k2.

ROW 6: K3, yo, ssk, * k6, yo, ssk; rep from *, end k2.

ROW 8: Knit.

ROW 10: K1, * k5, yo, sk2p, yo; rep from *, end k6.

ROW 12: K7, * yo, ssk, k6; rep from *.

87.   **EIFFEL TOWER EYELETS**

Other Name:

Raindrops.

General
Description:

This purl-fabric eyelet pattern is designed to be worked over a bed of reverse stockinette. The tiny towers are formed by knit stitches worked directly above the eyelet. The gaping hole created by the yarn-over widens the bottom of the knit-stitch tower, revealing the back side of the stitches and giving the pattern its name.

Properties: Though the fabric formed by this pattern has the same general properties as reverse stockinette— including good drape and moderate elasticity—its design creates two characteristics decidedly different from reverse stockinette: The fabric's surface has a raised texture, and a gaping hole sits at the bottom of each tower.

Yarn Consumption: The narrow strips of knit stitches on a bed of purl stitches draw in the fabric slightly, counteracting any opening effect of the eyelets and keeping yarn consumption approximately equal to stockinette.

Suggested Uses: This pattern would make for a dramatic sweater, as its design has distinct lines and a bold yet delicate texture. The towers resemble large tear-shaped beads. Try working the pattern into a funky tank in a yarn with excellent draping qualities, such as a rayon blend or mercerized cotton, for a unique top to wear out to the clubs.

2-8

Pattern: **(multiple of 6 stitches)**

ROW 1: * P4, yo, p2tog; rep from *.
ROWS 2, 4, AND 6: K1, * p1, k5; rep from *, end p1, k4.
ROWS 3 AND 5: P4, * k1, p5; rep from *, end k1, p1.
ROW 7: P1, * yo, p2tog, p4; rep from *, end yo, p2tog, p3.
ROWS 8, 10, AND 12: K4, * p1, k5; rep from *, end p1, k1.
ROWS 9 AND 11: P1, * k1, p5; rep from *, end k1, p4.

88. **DAISY EYELETS**

Other Name: Flower eyelets.

General Description: A simple arrangement of six eyelets around a central eyelet, this pattern dates back several centuries and owes its enduring popularity to its straightforward patterning and classic appearance.

Properties: The fabric alternates between solid patches of stockinette stitch and open patches of eyelets, which cover roughly equal surface area. The stockinette gives it some substance, and the eyelet flowers lend increased drape and airiness.

Yarn
Consumption:

Suggested Uses:
0–6

The large clumps of eyelets open up the fabric enough to decrease yarn usage.

The openness created by the eyelet flowers make this pattern suitable for projects intended to be worn over other garments, such as summer cardigans, baby sweaters, or baby blankets.

Pattern:

NOTE: All yarn-overs are double ones, written "yo2" instead of the usual "(yo) twice."

ROW 1: K10, * k2tog, ssk, k12; rep from *, end last repeat k10.

ROW 2 AND ALL OTHER WRONG-SIDE ROWS: Purl, working (k1, p1) into every double yo.

ROW 3: K8, * (k2tog, yo2, ssk) twice, k8; rep from *.

ROW 5: Repeat Row 1.

ROW 7: Repeat Row 3.

ROW 9: Repeat Row 1.

ROW 11: K2, * k2tog, yo2, ssk, k12; rep from *, end (k2tog, yo2, ssk) twice.

ROW 13: * (K2tog, yo2, ssk) twice, k8; rep from *, end (k2tog, yo2, ssk) twice.

ROW 15: Repeat Row 11.

ROW 17: Repeat Row 13.

ROW 19: Repeat Row 11.

ROW 20: See Row 2.

89.   **BRAIDED EYELETS**

Other Names: Butterfly braid, braided lace panel.

General
Description: A two-dimensional braiding of three eyelet strips, this
pattern looks like a cubist portrayal of the open syncopated cable.

Properties: The fabric has strips of double eyelets separated by
solid blocks of stockinette. The stockinette areas anchor
the fabric and give it some substance, while the eyelet
strips give the fabric significantly increased drape.

Yarn
Consumption: The long, continuous lines of eyelets open up the fabric
and decrease yarn consumption considerably.

Suggested Uses: Not only would this pattern be an excellent border
 0–6   for a stole, it would also make an attractive panel
inserted into any sweater or down the side of a lined
skirt. Try knitting it in the round to make an unusual
pair of children's stockings.

Pattern: **(panel of 22 stitch)**

ROW 1 (WS) AND ALL OTHER WRONG-SIDE ROWS:
Purl.
ROW 2: K5, (yo, ssk) twice, k3, (k2tog, yo) twice, k6.
ROW 4: K3, (k2tog, yo) twice, k4, (k2tog, yo) twice,
k1, yo, ssk, k4.

ROW 6: K2, (k2tog, yo) twice, k4, (k2tog, yo) twice, k1, (yo, ssk) twice, k3.

ROW 8: K1, (k2tog, yo) twice, k4, (k2tog, yo) twice, k3, (yo, ssk) twice, k2.

ROW 10: K3, (yo, ssk) twice, k1, (k2tog, yo) twice, k5, (yo, ssk) twice, k1.

ROW 12: K4, yo, ssk, yo, sk2p, yo, k2tog, yo, k4, (k2tog, yo) twice, k3.

ROW 14: K5, yo, ssk, yo, sk2p, yo, k4, (k2tog, yo) twice, k4.

ROW 16: K6, (yo, ssk) twice, k3, (k2tog, yo) twice, k5.

ROW 18: K4, k2tog, yo, k1, (yo, ssk) twice, k4, (yo, ssk) twice, k3.

ROW 20: K3, (k2tog, yo) twice, k1, (yo, ssk) twice, k4, (yo, ssk) twice, k2.

ROW 22: K2, (k2tog, yo) twice, k3, (yo, ssk) twice, k4, (yo, ssk) twice, k1.

ROW 24: K1, (k2tog, yo) twice, k5, (yo, ssk) twice, k1, (k2tog, yo) twice, k3.

ROW 26: K3, (yo, ssk) twice, k4, yo, ssk, yo, k3tog, yo, k2tog, yo, k4.

ROW 28: K4, (yo, ssk) twice, k4, yo, k3tog, yo, k2tog, yo, k5.

90a–b.

CABLED EYELETS

General Description: The cable in this pattern is created by passing a slipped stitch over two knit stitches, which pinches the fabric and gives the small-scale pattern the appearance of a cable crossing. A yarn-over is worked in the rows between each decrease to restore the original number of stitches, simultaneously creating a hole in the fabric.

Properties:

The slipped stitches and yarn-overs give the fabric texture. Working decreases and increases on alternating rows creates uneven tension that pulls in and pushes out the fabric, giving each column rounded edges.

Yarn Consumption:

The yarn-overs open up the fabric, but the effect is mitigated by the pinching of the decreases, so the pattern uses approximately the same amount of yarn as stockinette.

Suggested Uses:

0–8

The pattern is easy to work and creates an interesting, small-scale cable-rib effect, which would be wonderful in a summer blouse. Try working a six-inch band around a fitted waist—the pattern creates a delicate gathering that adds interest without adding significant bulk, and its vertical lines are flattering on any figure.

Pattern:

(multiple of 6 stitches)

ROW 1: * Sl 1, k2, pass slipped stitch over the 2 knit stitches, k3; rep from *.
ROW 2: P4, * yo, p5; rep from *, end yo, p1.

ROW 3: * K3, sl 1, k2, pass slipped stitch over the 2 knit stitches; rep from *.

ROW 4: P1, * yo, p5; rep from *, end yo, p4.

Variation: *Lace Diamond Chain* (panel of 18 stitches)

This pattern teeters on the line between eyelet pattern and lace; the eyelets are separated by a single strand of yarn but placed on a background of solid stockinette. The pattern is considered a variation to cabled eyelets because two yarn-over-outlined bands of stockinette cross over each other like simple cables.

ROW 1 (WS) AND ALL OTHER WRONG-SIDE ROWS: Purl.

ROW 2: K6, yo, ssk, k2, yo, ssk, k6.

ROW 4: K4, k2tog, yo, k1, yo, ssk, k2, yo, ssk, k5.

ROW 6: K3, k2tog, yo, k3, yo, ssk, k2, yo, ssk, k4.

ROW 8: (K2, k2tog, yo) twice, k1, yo, ssk, k2, yo, ssk, k3.

ROW 10: K1, k2tog, yo, k2, k2tog, yo, k3, (yo, ssk, k2) twice.

ROW 12: K3, yo, ssk, k2, yo, ssk, yo, k2tog, yo, k2, k2tog, yo, k2tog, k1.

ROW 14: K4, yo, ssk, k2, yo, sk2p, yo, k2, k2tog, yo, k3.

ROW 16: K5, yo, ssk, k2, yo, ssk, k1, k2tog, yo, k4.

91. 📷 **CAT'S EYE**

Other Names: Cat's eyelet.

General
Description: The cat's eye stitch pattern is an openwork pattern traditionally used to fill background spaces and create complementary edgings in lace shawl knitting. Examples of the stitch can be found in historic shawls from Ireland, Scotland, and Wales. The uniformly spaced double yarn-overs create a pattern that sets off more intricate lace openwork beautifully.

Properties: As a result of its double yarn-overs, cat's eye creates a
↔ textured, durable mesh with excellent drape and stretch in all directions.

Yarn
Consumption: The allover eyelets open up the fabric considerably, decreasing yarn consumption noticeably.

Suggested Uses: Aside from lace shawls, cat's eye might be employed
╲ 0–6 artfully in the design of a knit top—the mesh is thick enough to provide some coverage and warmth, and the texture would add visual interest to the project. It would also be suited for use in boleros, caps, wrist warmers, and other decorative accessories.

Pattern: **(multiple of 4 stitches, minimum of 12 stitches)**

ROW 1: K4, * (yo) twice, k4; rep from * to end.

ROW 2: P2, *p2tog, (p1, k1) into double yo of previous row, p2tog; rep from *, end p2.

ROW 3: K2, yo, *k4, (yo) twice; rep from * to last 6 sts, k4, yo, k2.

ROW 4: P3, * (p2tog) twice, (p1, k1) into double yo of previous row, rep from *, end (p2tog) twice, p3.

92. 📷   **GRAND EYELET LACE**

General Description:

The super-sized holes in this pattern are created by working three stitches into a single yarn-over. The design is more interesting than its name lets on—the alternating rows of eyelets look like strings of ringing bells or a large choir of hooded monks.

Properties:

This pattern forms a gaping, meshlike fabric with considerable drape and minimal structure.

Yarn Consumption:

The allover pattern of grand eyelets opens the fabric substantially, decreasing yarn consumption significantly.

Suggested Uses:

The interesting, yet simple, pattern would make this a good choice for a quick and easy fishnet-esque wrap worked in medium-weight yarn. Also consider incorporating a few rows along a sweater's edge or a single row to separate the border from the body of a lightweight lap blanket.

Pattern: **(multiple of 4 stitches + 4)**

⚠

NOTE: Row 3 should be worked very loosely, preferably using a needle 3 or 4 sizes larger than the needles used for the rest of the work.

ROW 1: P2, * yo, p4tog; rep from *, end p2.

ROW 2: K2, * k1, (k1, p1, k1) into the yo of the previous row; rep from *, end k2.

ROW 3: Knit.

93a–b. 📷 **CAT'S PAW**

Other Names: Crown of glory.

General Description: This traditional Shetland pattern uses a triple yarn-over to create the large, gaping hole that forms the base of each crown.

Properties: While the large swaths of stockinette surrounding each crown give the fabric substance and structure, the grand eyelet formed by the triple yarn-over spans the length of five knit stitches, opening up the fabric significantly and increasing its drape.

Yarn Consumption: The large holes at the center of each pattern repeat open up the fabric considerably, decreasing yarn consumption.

Suggested Uses:

A team-themed jersey for a sports lover would be a fun application of this pattern, as its generic paw could be used to represent any feline mascot (Go Cats! Lions! Tigers! Leopards! Tabbys!). But traditional Shetland shawls, knit at a very fine gauge, are best suited to this eyelet pattern.

Pattern:

(multiple of 14 stitches + 5)

ROW 1: K3, * ssk, k9, k2tog, k1; rep from *, end k2.
ROW 2: P2, * p1, p2tog, p7, p2tog tbl, rep from *, end p3.
ROW 3: K3, * ssk, k2, (yo) 3 times, k3, k2tog, k1; rep from *, end k2.
ROW 4: P2, * p1, p2tog, p2; make 5 sts out of the large loop formed by 3 yos of previous row by working (k1, p1) twice, k1 into it; p1, p2tog tbl; repeat from *, end p3.
ROW 5: K3, * ssk, k6, k2tog, k1; rep from *, end k2.
ROW 6: P2, * p1, p2tog, p6; rep from *, end p3.
ROW 7: K3, k1, (yo, k1) 6 times, k1; rep from *, end k2.
ROW 8: Purl.
ROWS 9 AND 11: Knit.
ROWS 10 AND 12: Purl.

Variation: *Traditional Cat's Paw* (multiple of 11 stitches)
In this much smaller pattern, six eyelets are clustered around knit stitches in a vertical band, traditionally used as a border strip in Shetland shawls.

ROW 1: K3, ssk, yo, k1, yo, k2tog, k3.
ROW 2 AND ALL OTHER WRONG-SIDE ROWS: Purl.
ROW 3: K2, ssk, yo, k3, yo, k2tog, k2.
ROW 5: K4, yo, s2kp, yo, k4.
ROW 6: Purl.

94. 📷 **FAGGOT CHECK**

Other Name: Lace check.

General
Description:
Faggoting is the most basic type of lace stitch, and the term refers to any stitch pattern in which a yarn-over/decrease combination is worked multiple times side by side. In this pattern, square panels of faggot stitch are inserted into a field of stockinette to create a check pattern.

Properties:
↔
Squares of stockinette are bordered by squares of lace faggoting and vice versa; when netted together, this gives the fabric a fair amount of drape and increased elasticity.

Yarn
Consumption:
The large blocks of faggoting open up the fabric, decreasing yarn consumption.

Suggested Uses:
\ 0–6
Try this pattern as the center motif in a square shawl, or knit a long strip of this pattern for a geometrically themed table runner and border it with another cabled eyelet stitch or Flemish blocks.

Pattern: **(multiple of 18 stitches + 9)**

ROW 1 (WS) AND ALL OTHER WRONG-SIDE ROWS: Purl.
ROWS 2, 6, AND 10: K1, * (yo, k2tog) 4 times, k10;
    rep from *, end (yo, k2tog) 4 times.
ROWS 4, 8, AND 12: * (Ssk, yo) 4 times, k10; rep from *,
    end last repeat k1.
ROWS 14, 18, AND 22: * K10, (yo, k2tog) 4 times; rep
    from *, end k9.
ROWS 16, 20, AND 24: K9, * (ssk, yo) 4 times, k10;
    rep from *.

---

95.   **FAGGOTED ZIGZAG**

Other Name: Rib fantastic.

General
Description: This pattern takes advantage of the natural left- and
    right-biases created by the ssk and k2tog decreases.
    Vertical strips of faggoting are knit alternating between
    the two decreases to form a zigzag, which is bordered
    by bands of stockinette.

Properties: The fabric is very open, with increased vertical and
    horizontal stretch. When knit flat, the bias will pre-
    vent the edges of the fabric from forming a straight
    line. Instead the edges form a zigzag.

Yarn
Consumption:

The wide strips of faggoting open up the fabric significantly, decreasing yarn consumption substantially.

Suggested Uses:
0–6

While this would make an interesting border along the edge of a shawl or stole, a single panel inserted along the top of a sleeve would also spice up a sweater nicely.

Pattern:

(multiple of 11 stitches + 12)

ROW 1 (WS) AND ALL OTHER WRONG-SIDE ROWS:
Purl.
RIGHT-SIDE ROWS FROM 2 THROUGH 12: K2, * (yo, k2tog) 4 times, k3; rep from *, end last repeat, k2.
RIGHT-SIDE ROWS FROM 14 THROUGH 24: K2, * (ssk, yo) 4 times, k3; rep from *, end last repeat, k2.

96a–c.

FAGGOTED TRELLIS

Other Name:

Vertical lace trellis.

General
Description:

By alternating between left- and right-leaning decreases every other row, this pattern reduces the bias used by the faggoted zigzag to the smallest possible scale. The trellis pattern is formed by diagonally stacked columns of yarn-overs, which are bordered by crooked, vertical lines of knit stitches.

Properties:
↔

This pattern creates an even-tensioned mesh with excellent drape and substantial elasticity.

Yarn Consumption:
📖

This allover yarn-over pattern opens up the fabric significantly, decreasing yarn consumption substantially.

Suggested Uses:
╲ 0–6

Worked in long strips over a few rows, this would make an excellent simple border stitch for stoles or shawls. It also works beautifully as a background stitch or a filler stitch when used with other lace or traveling stitch patterns.

Pattern:

(odd number of stitches)

ROWS 1 AND 3 (WS): Purl.
ROW 2: K1, * yo, k2tog; rep from *.
ROW 4: * Ssk, yo; rep from *, end k1.

Variations:

Lace Trellis
Decreases are not alternated. A bias is formed in either direction, which will give the fabric a distinct slant.

Lace Trellis R (even number of stitches)
ROW 1: K1, * yo, k2tog; rep from *, end k1.
ROW 2: Purl.

Lace Trellis L (even number of stitches)
ROW 1: K1, * ssk, yo; rep from *, end k1.
ROW 2: Purl.

Faggoted Trellis Zigzag or *Zigzag Lace Trellis* (even number of stitches)

Two basic lace trellis patterns are switched every six rows. Try switching the number of rows each pattern is worked over to create a crazy zigzag.

ROW 1 (WS) AND ALL OTHER WRONG-SIDE ROWS: Purl.
ROWS 2, 4, AND 6: K1, * yo, k2tog; rep from *, end k1.
ROWS 8, 10, AND 12: K1, * ssk, yo; rep from *, end k1.

97a–b.

HERRINGBONE FAGGOT

General
Description:

This pattern combines narrow strips of faggoting with narrow strips of stockinette to form a pronounced ribbing pattern. Herringbone is applied to any faggoting pattern in which the faggot stitch of (yo, k2tog) is alternated with a single or double line of knit stitches to create vertical ribbing. With the limited number of elements, the number of existing herringbone faggot variations is surprising.

Properties:
↔

This pattern creates a textured, openwork ribbing with increased elasticity due to the yarn-overs. The drape is comparable to stockinette, and the vertical strips of knit stitches help the fabric retain some structure.

Yarn
Consumption:

The vertical strips of yarn-overs open up this fabric and increase its lateral stretch, decreasing yarn consumption.

Suggested Uses:

0–6

This pattern would make for very interesting, if not-quite-functional, socks. Stockings might be a better choice, as this pattern would give them a ribbed fishnet look. For something a bit more practical, try herringbone faggot as a ribbed cuff on a sweater sleeve—it would be particularly attractive on a short-sleeved summer blouse.

Pattern:

(multiple of 4 stitches)

ALL ROWS: * K2tog, yo, k2; rep from *.

Variation:

Herringbone Lace (multiple of 6 stitches + 2)
This pattern is a true 4x2 rib, with faggoting inserted every fourth row. The yarn-overs create some diagonal shaping on the knit bands.

ROW 1: P1, * p1, yo, ssk, k2tog, yo, p1; rep from *, end p1.
ROW 2: K1, * k1, p4, k1; rep from *, end k1.
ROW 3: P1, * p1, k4, p1; rep from *, end p1.
ROW 4: K1, * k1, p4, k1; rep from *, end k1.

98. 📷 **DOUBLE HERRINGBONE FAGGOT**

General
Description:

This pattern doubles the amount of times the faggot stitch is worked and reduces the number of knit stitches to one, creating a wider, less substantial version of its base stitch, the herringbone faggot.

Properties:
↔

This pattern creates a textured, openwork ribbing with increased elasticity due to its double strips of yarn-overs. It has excellent drape, and the single lines of knit stitches barely keep the fabric from being classified as mesh.

Yarn
Consumption:

The vertical strips of yarn-overs open up the fabric and increase its lateral stretch, decreasing yarn consumption.

Suggested Uses:
\ 0–6

The delicate rib pattern would be a very pretty edging for the bottom of a skirt. The practical-minded could knit this into a covering for a small window—it will block the neighbors' view while letting the sun shine through.

Pattern:

(multiple of 5 stitches)

ALL ROWS: * K1, (yo, k2tog) twice; rep from *.

99. 📷 **PURSE STITCH**

General
Description:
A close cousin to herringbone faggot stitch patterns, purse stitch chooses to purl two stitches together, rather than knit, because it prefers the increased elasticity generated by the greater distance between the yarn-over and subsequent purl stitch. It values flexibility—it's just that kind of stitch.

Properties:
↔
As noted in the stitch's bio, the delicate and uniform mesh formed by purse stitch is extremely elastic. It also has excellent draping qualities.

Yarn
Consumption:
🗄
The allover yarn-overs draw open the fabric considerably, decreasing yarn consumption significantly.

Suggested Uses:
╲ 0–6
This pattern would be the perfect border within a lace project to separate and offset more complicated lace patterns. However, the stitch's affinity for lace projects shouldn't overshadow its other assets, such as its net-like mesh. Consider using it for small basketball nets to hang over the recycling bin in the office—make recycling fun again.

Pattern:
(multiple of 2 stitches)

ALL ROWS: K1, * yo, p2tog; rep from *, end k1.

100. **LACE CHEVRON**

General
Description:

Like a child's rendering of birds flying across the sky, these eyelet Vs soar across the fabric in perfect formation.

Properties:

The fabric formed by this pattern shares many of the qualities of its base stitch, stockinette, such as good drape and moderate elasticity. However, the horizontal strips of eyelets give it an airiness and delicacy not found in solid fabrics.

Yarn
Consumption:

The solid lines of eyelets open up the fabric, decreasing yarn consumption.

Suggested Uses:

0–6h

This pattern would make a nice summer sweater or tank. Its patterning is not horizontal enough to detract from the wearer, and the eyelets would lend an airiness appropriate for the season.

Pattern:

(multiple of 10 stitches + 1)

ROW 1 (WS) AND ALL OTHER WRONG-SIDE ROWS:
Purl.
ROW 2: * K5, yo, ssk, k3; rep from *, end k1.
ROW 4: * K3, k2tog, yo, k1, yo, ssk, k2; rep from *, end k1.
ROW 6: * K2, k2tog, yo, k3, yo, ssk, k1; rep from *, end k1.
ROW 8: * K1, k2tog, yo, k5, yo, ssk; rep from *, end k1.

ROW 10: K2tog, yo, k7, * yo, sk2p, yo, k7; rep from
*, end yo, ssk.

101.   **LACE FEATHER**

General
Description:
This traditional Shetland lace pattern is formed by
pairing two yarn-overs with decreases on either side of
the pair, then repeating the progression every second
or fourth row to create a stack of holes that resemble,
well, a feather.

Properties:
While the yarn-overs give the fabric some airiness, the
solid vertical strips of stockinette and garter stitch ribs
lend it structure and texture. The ribs every fourth row
reduce the fabric's drape slightly; they can easily be
replaced with stockinette for a smoother fabric.

Yarn
Consumption:
The vertical lines of eyelets open up the fabric,
decreasing yarn consumption.

Suggested Uses:
In the British Isles, this pattern was traditionally used
as a color band or border stitch in lace shawls, but its
textural interest also makes it a fun choice for a sweater
sleeve or a handbag.

Pattern:
(multiple of 7 stitches)

ROWS 1 AND 3 (WS): Purl.

ROW 2: Knit.

ROW 4: * P1, p2tog, yo, k1, yo, p2tog, p1; rep from *.

102. **HORSESHOES**

General
Description:

Horseshoes is also a traditional lace pattern of the British Isles, named for its clever use of increases and decreases to curve bands of knit stitches up to a central rounded point.

Properties:

The fabric shares many qualities with its base stitch, stockinette, such as good drape and moderate elasticity. However, the vertical strip of double decreases at the center of each pattern repeat increases the fabric's structure and counteracts the airiness of the yarn-overs.

Yarn
Consumption:

The solid lines of eyelets open up the fabric, decreasing yarn consumption.

Suggested Uses:

0–6

This pattern is another traditionally used as a color-band or border stitch in Scottish, Irish, and Welsh lace. It would also be a very pretty as edging for a skirt or knit into a strip to sew onto the edge of a pillowcase.

Pattern:

(multiple of 10 stitches + 2)

ROW 1 (WS) AND ALL OTHER WRONG-SIDE ROWS: Purl.

ROW **2:** K1, * yo, k3, s2kp, k3, yo, k1; rep from *, end k1.

ROW **4:** K1, * k1, yo, k2, s2kp, k2, yo, k2; rep from *, end k1.

ROW **6:** K1, * k2, yo, k1, s2kp, k3, yo, k3; rep from *, end k1.

ROW **8:** K1, * k3, yo, s2kp, yo, k4; rep from *, end k1.

103. 📷 **TRELLIS LACE**

General Description:

More solid than its faggoted cousins, this stitch features vertical yarn-over trellis strips separated by four knit stitches, giving room to highlight the texture created by the alternating decreases.

Properties:

Despite its allover eyelet design, this pattern creates a fairly solid fabric with excellent drape and no bias. The trellis patterning is formed by the stacked yarn-overs and is accentuated by the raised diagonal stitches of the decreases.

Yarn Consumption:

The vertical strips of eyelets open up the fabric, decreasing yarn consumption.

Suggested Uses:

0–6

The interesting texture is magnified when worked over several repeats—as in a stole's central motif or a sweater's allover pattern—but a single repeat of this pattern also lends an understated elegance to any project when inserted as an accent or a border.

Pattern: **(multiple of 6 stitches + 5)**

ROW 1: K4, * yo, sk2p, yo, k3; rep from *, end k1.
ROW 2: Purl.
ROW 3: K1, * yo, sk2p, yo, k3; rep from *, end yo,
    sk2p, yo, k1.
ROW 4: Purl.

104. **LATTICE LACE**

General
Description:

This pattern makes excellent use of right- and left-
leaning decreases to form lattice laths crisscrossing
over the surface of the fabric. The yarn-overs counter-
act the thickened texture of the decreases, giving the
fabric a wonderful three-dimensional quality.

Properties:

This pattern forms a textured fabric, with excellent
drape and significant lateral stretch.

Yarn
Consumption:

The horizontal strips of yarn-overs open up the fabric,
decreasing yarn consumption slightly.

Suggested Uses:

The curvy outlines would pair up nicely with other
rounded lace patterns, such as falling leaves or flickering
flame lace, in a lace stole. Also consider using this
stitch in a lacy sock pattern.

Pattern: **(multiple of 7 stitches + 2)**

ROW 1: K3, * k2tog, yo, k5; rep from *, end last
repeat k4.
ROW 2: P2, * p2tog tbl, yo, p1, yo, p2tog, p2; rep from *.
ROW 3: K1, * k2tog, yo, k3, yo, skp; rep from *, end k1.
ROW 4: Purl.
ROW 5: K1, * yo, skp, k5; rep from *, end k1.
ROW 6: *P1, yo, p2tog, p2, p2tog tbl, yo; rep from *
to last 2 sts, p2.
ROW 7: * K3, yo, skp, k2tog, yo; rep from * to last
2 sts, k2.
ROW 8: Purl.

105a–b. 📷 **LACE SCALES**

Other Name: Milanese lace.

General
Description: This striking version of lacy scales is from Milan.
With every row, an additional knit stitch is inserted
between the decrease and yarn-over to curve the
stockinette blocks and send a bold diagonal line
across the fabric.

Properties: This pattern forms nonbiased, even-tensioned fabric,
with excellent drape and some texture. When the pattern
is worked in the round, the diagonal strips will form
spirals, which may or may not be desirable.

Yarn Consumption:	The yarn-overs that separate each lace scale increase the fabric's lateral spread, decreasing yarn consumption.
Suggested Uses:	Worked in a fine yarn, this pattern would make a beautifully unique shawl or stole.

Pattern: **(multiple of 6 stitches + 2)**

ROW 1: K1, * k4, k2tog, yo; rep from *, end k1.
ROW 2: P1, * yo, p1, p2tog, p3; rep from *, end p1.
ROW 3: K1, * k2, k2tog, k2, yo; rep from *, end k1.
ROW 4: P1, * yo, p3, p2tog, p1; rep from *, end p1.
ROW 5: K1, * k2tog, k4, yo; rep from *, end k1.
ROW 6: P2, * p4, yo, p2tog; rep from *.
ROW 7: K1, * k1, yo, k3, k2tog; rep from *, end k1.
ROW 8: P1, * p2tog, p2, yo, p2; rep from *, end p1.
ROW 9: K1, * k3, yo, k1, k2tog; rep from *, end k1.
ROW 10: P1, * p2tog, yo, p4; rep from *, end p1.

Variation: *Fish-Scale Lace* (panel of 17 stitches)
This pattern forms an attractive panel of overlapping fishtails (not scales) split down the middle, as seen in drawings of mermaids. A small triangle of purl stitches, resembling scales, sits at the top of each tail.

ROW 1: K1, yo, k3, skp, p5, k2tog, k3, yo, k1.
ROW 2: P6, k5, p6.
ROW 3: K2, yo, k3, skp, p3, k2tog, k3, yo, k2.
ROW 4: P7, k3, p7.

ROW 5: K3, yo, k3, skp, p1, k2tog, k3, yo, k3.
ROW 6: P8, k1, p8.
ROW 7: K4, yo, k3, sk2p, k3, yo, k4.
ROW 8: Purl.

106. **FALLING LEAVES**

General
Description:
This well-known openwork lace pattern is differentiated from basic leaf patterns because its leaves are worked upside-down and separated by strips of yarn-overs to give the impression that they are scattering in the wind.

Properties:
Because the leaves are floating in pools of yarn-overs, this pattern forms a lightly textured fabric with a very loose drape and little structure.

Yarn
Consumption:
Despite the solid stockinette leaves, the yarn-overs open up the fabric considerably, decreasing yarn consumption.

Suggested Uses:
0–6
A favorite in triangular shawls, this pattern's diagonal sides make it easy to insert increases and additional stitch repeats. The extremely loose fabric is not suitable for any garment requiring inherent structure.

Pattern:
(multiple of 10 stitches + 6)

ROW 1 (WS) AND ALL OTHER WRONG-SIDE ROWS:
Purl.

ROW 2: K1, yo, * k3, s2kp, k3, yo, k1, yo; rep from *, end k3, k2tog.

ROW 4: K2, * yo, k2, s2kp, k2, yo, k3; rep from *, end yo, k2, k2tog.

ROW 6: K2, * k1, yo, k1, s2kp, k1, yo, k4; rep from *, end k1, yo, k1, k2tog.

ROW 8: K2, * k2, yo, s2kp, yo, k5; rep from *, end k2, yo, k2tog.

ROW 10: Ssk, k1, * k2, yo, k1, yo, k3, s2kp, k1; rep from *, end k2, yo, k1.

ROW 12: Ssk, k1, * k1, yo, k3, yo, k2, s2kp, k1; rep from *, end k1, yo, k2.

ROW 14: Ssk, k1, * yo, k5, yo, k1, s2kp, k1; rep from *, end yo, k3.

ROW 16: Ssk, yo, * k7, yo, s2kp, yo; rep from *, end k4.

107. 📷 **STAGGERED LEAVES**

Other Names: Staggered fern lace, diagonal fern lace.

General Description: This pattern combines two staggered strips of leaves to give the impression that a plant is growing up and outward—the decreases' natural bias curve the "leaves" around and up, reinforcing the yarn-over pattern within each leaf.

Properties: The fairly solid fabric is punctuated by short diagonal strips of paired yarn-overs. The staggered decreases create a bias, which forces the edges of the fabric to scallop inward.

Yarn Consumption:

Despite the solid stockinette leaves, the yarn-overs increase the fabric's lateral spread, decreasing yarn consumption.

Suggested Uses:

This pattern is worked on a background of garter stitch, but reverse stockinette could easily be substituted for a different look.

Pattern:

(multiple of 18 stitches + 2)

ROW 1 (WS) AND ALL OTHER WRONG-SIDE ROWS: Purl.
ROW 2: P2, * k9, yo, k1, yo, k3, sk2p, p2; rep from *.
ROW 4: P2, * k10, yo, k1, yo, k2, sk2p, p2; rep from *.
ROW 6: P2, * k3tog, k4, yo, k1, yo, k3, (yo, k1) twice, sk2p, p2; rep from *.
ROW 8: P2, * k3tog, k3, yo, k1, yo, k9, p2; rep from *.
ROW 10: P2, * k3tog, k2, yo, k1, yo, k10, p2; rep from *.
ROW 12: P2, * k3tog, (k1, yo) twice, k3, yo, k1, yo, k4, sk2p, p2; rep from *.

108.

FLICKERING FLAMES

General Description:

This intriguing pattern is a variation of standard leaf patterns: There are paired yarn-overs at the base of each flame, but the top-half decreases are worked in the center of each flame rather than along the outside edge. Therefore, the edge of each flame blends into the next, giving the pattern the shimmering effect for which it is named.

Properties: This pattern creates an even-tensioned, fairly solid fabric with a lightly textured surface and excellent drape.

Yarn
Consumption: Despite the solid stockinette leaves, the yarn-overs increase the fabric's lateral spread and decrease yarn consumption.

Suggested Uses: This pattern's drape and compelling design make it an
0–6 ideal choice for a shawl.

Pattern: **(multiple of 10 stitches + 1)**

ROWS 1, 3, 5 AND 7: K1, * yo, k3, sk2p, k3, yo, k1; rep from *.
ROWS 2, 4, 6, AND 8: Purl.
ROWS 9, 11, 13, AND 15: K2tog, k3, yo, k1, yo, k3, *sk2p, k3, yo, k1, yo, k3; rep from * to last 2 sts, skp.
ROWS 10, 12, 14, AND 16: Purl.

---

109. **CANDLE FLAMES**

General
Description: This pattern forms a bold, embossed flame motif. With eight more rows in each repeat than the flickering

flames pattern, it creates significantly taller flames.

Properties:

The mostly solid fabric has good drape. The stockinette flames are separated by columns of purl stitches, which create a small ribbing effect. The uneven bias will also cause the edges of the fabric to wave in and out.

Yarn
Consumption:

The increased lateral stretch created by the yarn-overs is completely mitigated by the lateral pull of the reverse stockinette ribs between each vertical strip of flames, causing this pattern to use approximately the same amount of yarn as stockinette.

Suggested Uses:

 0–6

This would be a striking choice for a wrap; knitted into a long vertical strip, it would also make a gorgeous holiday table runner.

Pattern:

(multiple of 12 stitches + 2)

NOTE: The stitch count varies from row to row. Original count is restored on Rows 12 and 24.

ROW 1: * P2, yo, k1, yo, p2, k2, k2tog, k3; rep from *, end p2.

ROW 2: * K2, p6, k2, p3; rep from *, end k2.

ROW 3: * P2, k1, (yo, k1) twice, p2, k2, k2tog, k2; rep from *, end p2.

ROW 4: * (K2, p5) twice; rep from *, end k2.

ROW 5: * P2, k2, yo, k1, yo, k2, p2, k2, k2tog, k1; rep from *, end p2.

ROW 6: * K2, p4, k2, p7; rep from *, end k2.

ROW 7: * P2, k3, yo, k1, yo, k3, p2, k2, k2tog; rep from *, end p2.

ROW 8: * K2, p3, k2, p9; rep from *, end k2.

ROW 9: * P2, k2, k2tog, k5, p2, k1, k2tog; rep from *, end p2.

ROW 10: * K2, p2, k2, p8; rep from *, end k2.

ROW 11: * P2, k2, k2tog, k4, p2, k2tog; rep from *, end p2.

ROW 12: * K2, p1, k2, p7; rep from *, end k2.

ROW 13: * P2, k2, k2tog, k3, p2, yo, k1, yo; rep from *, end p2.

ROW 14: * K2, p3, k2, p6; rep from *, end k2.

ROW 15: * P2, k2, k2tog, k2, p2, (k1, yo) twice, k1; rep from *, end p2.

ROW 16: * (K2, p5) twice; rep from *, end k2.

ROW 17: * P2, k2, k2tog, k1, p2, k2, yo, k1, yo, k2; rep from *, end p2.

ROW 18: * K2, p7, k2, p4; rep from *, end k2.

ROW 19: * P2, k2, k2tog, p2, k3, yo, k1, yo, k3; rep from *, end p2.

ROW 20: * K2, p9, k2, p3; rep from *, end k2.

ROW 21: * P2, k1, k2tog, p2, k2, k2tog, k5; rep from *, end p2.

ROW 22: * K2, p8, k2, p2; rep from *, end k2.

ROW 23: * P2, k2tog, p2, k2, k2tog, k4; rep from *, end p2.

ROW 24: * K2, p7, k2, p1; rep from *, end k2.

110.   **BEECH LEAF**

General
Description:

This pattern creates a realistic rendering of paired leaves, stacked in a vertical column. Much like the falling leaves pattern, these leaves float on a bed of yarn-overs, giving each repeat definition and an air of looseness.

Properties:

The fabric lacks structure, despite its mostly stockinette leaves. Consequently, it has excellent drape and some subtle texture from the decreases on each leaf.

Yarn
Consumption:

Despite the stockinette leaves, the yarn-overs open up the fabric considerably and decrease yarn consumption.

Suggested Uses:

Its loose drape and defined edges would make this pattern a good choice as a shawl edging, although it would also look lovely worked into a summer blouse or a child's sweater.

0–6

Pattern:

(multiple of 14 stitches + 1)

NOTE: The stitch count does not remain consistent from row to row. Original count is restored on Rows 5–10.

ROW 1: * K1, yo, k5, yo, sk2p, yo, k5, yo; rep from *, end k1.

ROW 2: Purl.

ROW 3: * K1, yo, k1, k2tog, p1, ssk, k1, yo, p1, yo, k1, k2tog, p1, ssk, k1, yo; rep from *, end k1.

ROW 4: P1, * (p3, k1) 3 times, p4; rep from *.

ROW 5: * K1, yo, k1, k2tog, p1, ssk, k1, p1, k1, k2tog, p1, ssk, k1, yo; rep from *, end k1.

ROW 6: P1, * p3, k1, (p2, k1) twice, p4; rep from *.

ROW 7: * (K1, yo) twice, k2tog, p1, ssk, p1, k2tog, p1, ssk, yo, k1, yo; rep from *, end k1.

ROW 8: P1, * p4, (k1, p1) twice, k1, p5; rep from *.

ROW 9: * K1, yo, k3, yo, sk2p, p1, k3tog, yo, k3, yo; rep from *, end k1.

ROW 10: Purl.

---

111. 📷 **DROOPING ELM LEAF**

General Description:
Similar to the beech leaf pattern, here two leaves are paired, but staggered, in a vertical strip.

Properties:
The fabric has excellent drape and little structure. The uneven pairing of the leaves creates a small bias, which causes the fabric's edges to gently curve back and forth with each pattern and row repeat.

Yarn Consumption:
🧶🧶
Despite the solid stockinette leaves, the yarn-overs open up the fabric considerably and decrease yarn consumption.

Suggested Uses:
∖ 0–6
The defined edges and excellent drape make this pattern suitable for a shawl or stole's edge, but also think about using it as a center strip to divide different sections or motifs within a larger lace project.

Pattern: **(multiple of 15 stitches + 1)**

NOTE: In Rows 3 and 4, there will be one fewer stitch per repeat.

ROW 1: * K1, yo, k1, ssk, p1, k2tog, k1, yo, p1, ssk, p1, k2tog, yo, k1, yo; rep from *, end k1.

ROW 2: P1, * p4, k1, p1, k1, p3, k1, p4; rep from *.

ROW 3: * K1, yo, k1, ssk, p1, k2tog, k1, p1, sk2p, yo, k3, yo; rep from *, end k1.

ROW 4: P1, * p6, k1, p2, k1, p4; rep from *.

ROW 5: * (K1, yo) twice, ssk, p1, (k2tog) twice, yo, k5, yo; rep from *, end k1.

ROW 6: P1, * p7, k1, p1, k1, p5; rep from *.

ROW 7: * K1, yo, k3, yo, sk2p, p1, yo, k1, ssk, p1, k2tog, k1, yo; rep from *, end k1.

ROW 8: P1, * (p3, k1) twice, p7; rep from *.

ROW 9: * K1, yo, k5, yo, ssk, k1, ssk, p1, k2tog, k1, yo; rep from *, end k1.

ROW 10: P1, * p3, k1, p2, k1, p8; rep from *.

---

112. 📷 **DAYFLOWER LACE**

General Description: Keeping track of the different number of stitches in each row is well worth the prize of this pattern's complex and attractive appearance, which resembles a stylized version of the two-petal flower for which it is named.

Properties:

↔

The loosely structured fabric has excellent drape and a bias, which causes the vertical edges to curve gently in and out with each row repeat. Because the fabric's bottom edge is very unevenly tensioned, heavy blocking is needed to attain any semblance of a straight edge.

Yarn
Consumption:

🗄

The dayflower petals float in a wide strip of yarn-overs, which substantially increases the fabric's lateral stretch and decreases the yarn consumption.

Suggested Uses:

╲ 0–6

Dayflower lace would be beautiful as either an allover pattern or edging for a shawl or stole. A single panel would be a graceful addition to any sleeve, skirt, or bag.

Pattern:

⚠

(panel of 19 stitches or multiple of 17 stitches + 2)

ROW 1 (WS) AND ALL OTHER WRONG-SIDE ROWS EXCEPT ROWS 5 AND 13: Purl.

ROW 2: K2, yo, k2tog, yo, (k2tog) 3 times, k2, yo, k3, yo, ssk, yo, k2. (19 sts)

ROW 4: K2, yo, k2tog, (k3tog) twice, yo, k1, yo, k2, (ssk, yo) twice, k2. (17 sts)

ROW 5: P11, p2tog, p4. (16 sts)

ROW 6: K2, yo, k3tog, yo, k3, yo, k2, (ssk, yo) twice, k2. (17 sts)

ROW 8: K2, yo, k2tog, yo, k1, (yo, k2, ssk) twice, yo, ssk, yo, k2. (19 sts)

ROW 10: K2, yo, k2tog, yo, k3, yo, k2, (ssk) 3 times, yo, ssk, yo, k2. (19 sts)

ROW 12: K2, (yo, k2tog) twice, k2, yo, k1, yo, (sk2p) twice, ssk, yo, k2. (17 sts)

ROW 13: P4, p2tog-tbl, p11. (16 sts)

ROW 14: K2, (yo, k2tog) twice, k2, yo, k3, yo, sk2p, yo, k2. (17 sts)

ROW 16: K2, yo, k2tog, yo, (k2tog, k2, yo) twice, k1, yo, ssk, yo, k2. (19 sts)

113.

BEAD STITCH

General Description:

This pattern is named for the bumps generated by the p3tog worked every fourth row, but when the fabric is viewed from a distance, the beads are part of a larger series of interlocking vertical strips.

Properties:

The pattern creates a bumpy, textured fabric with structured vertical strips offset by valleys of yarn-overs.

Yarn Consumption:

The increased lateral stretch created by the yarn-overs is offset by the pull of the decreases, causing this pattern to use approximately the same amount of yarn as stockinette.

Suggested Uses: 0–6

Unless worked with a fine yarn, this pattern's eyelets may be hidden in the fabric's pull, making it a good choice for a thin sweater or interesting shrug.

Pattern:	**(multiple of 7 stitches)**

ROW 1 (WS): K1, k2tog, yo, k1, yo, skp, * k2, k2tog, yo, k1, yo, skp; rep from *, end k1.

ROW 2: * P2tog-tbl, yo, p3, yo, p2tog; rep from *.

ROW 3: K1, yo, skp, k1, k2tog, yo, * k2, yo, skp, k1, k2tog, yo; rep from *, end k1.

ROW 4: P2, yo, p3tog, yo, * p4, yo, p3tog, yo; rep from *, end p2.

114. **FOAMING WAVES**

Other Names:	Crest of the wave.
General Description:	This graphic pattern utilizes garter stitch bands to create "foam" along waving curves of stockinette and yarn-overs.
Properties:	The highly textured fabric has excellent drape. Vertical strips of stockinette and horizontal bands of garter stitch provide some structure, but this structure is mostly offset by the wide bands of yarn-overs. A light blocking will pop the foam ridge from the fabric, but avoid a heavy blocking.
Yarn Consumption:	The vertical bands of yarn-overs greatly increase the fabric's lateral stretch, decreasing yarn consumption.

Suggested Uses: Light-colored yarns show off this pattern best, though
it is interesting enough to look good in any color
yarn. The waves and texture would make this a fun
choice for a wrap. Also consider this pattern for an
unusual edging—its "foam" ridges double as mock
frilly ruffles.

Pattern: **(multiple of 12 stitches + 1)**

ROWS 1–4: Knit.
ROWS 5, 7, 9, AND 11 (RS): K1, * (k2tog) twice, (yo,
k1) 3 times, yo, (skp) twice, k1; rep from *.
ROWS 6, 8, 10, AND 12: Purl.

---

115. **SNOWDROPS**

General
Description:
Named for the delicate white flower with downward-
drooping petals, this traditional English lace pattern
forms a delicate, simple image of three-petal flowers
floating in a web of openwork.

Properties: This pattern creates an even-tensioned, openwork
fabric with minimal structure and excellent drape.

Yarn
Consumption:
Liberal use of yarn-overs opens up the fabric consider-
ably, decreasing yarn consumption substantially.

Suggested Uses:
\ 0–6

The simple elegance of this pattern lends itself to its traditional use as an allover pattern in lace shawls and stoles. Though the pattern's lack of structure makes it unsuitable for many garments, it could be considered for a loose, lacy cardigan or tank top.

Pattern:

(multiple of 8 stitches + 5)

ROW 1 (WS) AND ALL OTHER WRONG-SIDE ROWS: Purl.
ROW 2: K1, * k3, yo, ssk, k1, k2tog, yo; rep from *, end k4.
ROW 4: K1, * yo, sk2p, yo, k1, yo, sk2p, yo, k1; rep from *, end yo, sk2p, yo, k1.
ROWS 6 AND 8: K1, * yo, sk2p, yo, k5; rep from *, end yo, sk2p, yo, k1.

116.

FIR CONE

General
Description:

In this traditional lace pattern from the British Isles, right- and left-leaning decreases make lines of knit stitches radiate around centers of paired yarn-overs to create the image of a pinecone. Viewed differently, the strips of yarn-overs look like little ladybugs or turtles swimming in pools of stockinette.

Properties:
↔

The fairly solid fabric has excellent drape. The double decreases form tiny vertical ridges in the top center of each cone.

Yarn Consumption:

The groups of paired yarn-overs increase this pattern's lateral stretch, decreasing yarn consumption slightly.

Suggested Uses:

\ 0–6

Because it has more substance than many lace patterns while retaining excellent drape, this pattern is well suited for its traditional use as an allover stitch pattern in shawls and stoles. Also try it as a delicate yet warm pattern for a baby blanket.

Pattern:

(multiple of 10 stitches + 11)

ROW 1 (WS) AND ALL OTHER WRONG-SIDE ROWS: Purl.
ROWS 2, 4, 6, AND 8: K1, * yo, k3, sk2p, k3, yo, k1; rep from *, end yo, k3, sk2p, k3, yo, k1.
ROWS: 10, 12, 14, AND 16: K2tog, * k3, yo, k1, yo, k3, sk2p; rep from *, end k3, yo, k1, yo, k3, ssk.

117.

SWINGING TRIANGLES

Other Name:

Swing stitch.

General Description:

This geometric pattern consists of bold eyelet triangles that touch tip-to-tip for a diagonal, swinging effect.

Properties:

Yarn-overs give the fabric excellent drape and increased lateral stretch, while paired decreases create a subtle texture.

Yarn
Consumption:

Liberal use of yarn-overs opens up the fabric, decreasing yarn consumption noticeably.

Suggested Uses:
\ 0–6

The bold, geometric design would make this pattern a fun choice for a child's blouse or a lively neck scarf.

Pattern:

(multiple of 12 stitches + 1)

ROW 1 (WS) AND ALL OTHER WRONG-SIDE ROWS: Purl.

ROW 2: * K10, skp, yo, rep from * to last st, k1.

ROW 4: K9, skp, yo, * k10, skp, yo, rep from * to last 2 sts, k2.

ROW 6: * K8, (skp, yo) twice; rep from * to last st, k1.

ROW 8: K7, (skp, yo) twice, * k8, (skp, yo) twice; rep from * to last 2 sts, k2.

ROW 10: * K6, (skp, yo) 3 times; rep from * to last st, k1.

ROW 12: K5, (skp, yo) 3 times * k6, (skp, yo) 3 times; rep from * to last 2 sts, k2.

ROW 14: * K4, (skp, yo) 4 times; rep from * to last st, k1.

ROW 16: K1, * yo, k2tog, k10; rep from *.

ROW 18: K2, yo, k2tog, * k10, yo, k2tog; rep from * to last 9 sts, k9.

ROW 20: K1, * (yo, k2tog) twice, k8; rep from *.

ROW 22: K2, (yo, k2tog) twice, * k8, (yo, k2tog) twice; rep from * to last 7 sts, k7.

ROW 24: K1, * (yo, k2tog) 3 times, k6; rep from *.

ROW 26: K2, (yo, k2tog) 3 times, * k6, (yo, k2tog) 3

times; rep from * to last 5 sts, k5.

ROW 28: K1, * (yo, k2tog) 4 times, k4; rep from *.

118. **FEATHER AND FAN**

Other Name: Old shale.

General
Description:
This traditional Shetland lace pattern is famous for the simple way it forms the fabric into deep waves; its rolling rhythm is showcased particularly well when the color of the yarn is changed every few rows. The old shale name is believed to come from the patterns of the waves breaking on shale beaches.

Properties:
The textured fabric has deep scalloping along its horizontal edge and very slight scalloping along its vertical edge, mostly due to the garter stitch ridges poking out.

Yarn
Consumption:
The horizontal bands of yarn-overs increase the fabric's lateral stretch, decreasing yarn consumption noticeably.

Suggested Uses:
Though famous for its use in traditional Shetland shawls, the stitch's ruffled edges also make it a nice choice for edgings of any kind—shawls, skirts, necklines, or sleeves. It is also an excellent choice for socks, especially when worked in self-striping sock yarn colorways.

Pattern: **(multiple of 18 stitches)**

ROW 1: Knit.

ROW 2: Purl.

ROW 3: * (K2tog) 3 times, (yo, k1) 6 times, (k2tog) 3 times; rep from *.

ROW 4: Knit.

---

119. **SHETLAND FERN**

General Description: This traditional Shetland lace leaf panel bears a greater resemblance to the Madeira fan stitch than the traditional leaf patterns—its broad-based leaves are surrounded by yarn-overs and sit on a bed of stockinette.

Properties: This panel forms a lightly textured fabric with excellent drape and without bias in any direction.

Yarn Consumption: The yarn-overs increase the fabric's vertical and horizontal stretch, decreasing yarn consumption significantly.

Suggested Uses: The delicate pattern makes Shetland fern an excellent candidate for a border panel in any intricate lace project, including shawls, stoles, table runners, handkerchiefs, scarves, veils, or baby blankets.

Pattern: **(panel of 15 stitches)**

ROW 1: K7, yo, ssk, k6.
ROWS 2, 4, 6, 8, AND 10: Purl.
ROW 3: K5, k2tog, yo, k1, yo, ssk, k5.
ROW 5: K4, k2tog, yo, k3, yo, ssk, k4.
ROW 7: K4, yo, ssk, yo, sk2p, yo, k2tog, yo, k4.
ROW 9: K2, k2tog, yo, k1, yo, ssk, k1, k2tog, yo, k1, yo, ssk, k2.
ROW 11: K2, (yo, ssk) twice, k3, (k2tog, yo) twice, k2.
ROW 12: P3, (yo, p2tog) twice, p1, (p2tog-tbl, yo) twice, p3.
ROW 13: K4, yo, ssk, yo, sk2p, yo, k2tog, yo, k4.
ROW 14: P5, yo, p2tog, p1, p2tog-tbl, yo, p5.
ROW 15: K6, yo, s2kp, yo, k6.
ROW 16: Purl.

---

120. **MADEIRA FAN**

Other Name: Madeira cascade.

General
Description:
This pattern dates back centuries and is renowned for its crisp lines and bold pattern. The island of Madeira is noted for its artisan embroidery, and many lace patterns have emulated the region's distinct style by incorporating strong vertical or diagonal lines into their designs.

Properties:

This lightly textured fabric has excellent drape, and the biased decreases form a deep scalloping along the fabric's lower edge.

Yarn Consumption:

The yarn-overs in this pattern draw out the fabric, decreasing yarn consumption.

Suggested Uses: 0–6

Use this pattern's scalloped lower edge to create interest at the hem of a skirt or blouse. Knitters with a triangle fetish may consider pairing this stitch with the swinging triangle pattern to create a geometrically themed shawl.

Pattern:

(multiple of 20 stitches + 5)

ROW 1: Purl.

ROW 2: Knit.

ROW 3: K2, * k1, yo, k8, sk2p, k8, yo; rep from *, end k3.

WRONG-SIDE ROWS FROM 4–18: Purl.

ROW 5: K2, * k2, yo, k7, sk2p, k7, yo, k1; rep from *, end k3.

ROW 7: K2, k2tog, * yo, k1, yo, k6, sk2p, k6, yo, k1, yo, sk2p; rep from *, end last repeat yo, ssk, k2.

ROW 9: K2, * k4, yo, k5, sk2p, k5, yo, k3; rep from *, end k3.

ROW 11: K2, * k1, yo, sk2p, yo, k1, yo, k4, sk2p, k4, yo, k1, yo, sk2p, yo; rep from *, end k3.

ROW 13: K2, * k6, yo, k3, sk2p, k3, yo, k5; rep from *, end k3.

ROW 15: K2, k2tog, * yo, k1, yo, sk2p, yo, k1, yo, k2, sk2p, k2, (yo, k1, yo, dd) twice; rep from *, end last repeat yo, ssk, k2.

ROW 17: K2, * k8, yo, k1, sk2p, k1, yo, k7; rep from *, end k3.

ROW 19: K2, * (k1, yo, sk2p, yo) 5 times; rep from *, end k3.

ROW 20: Knit.

---

121. **BIRD'S EYE**

General Description:
An ancient Shetland mesh pattern, this stitch is a touch more delicate than cat's eye, since the knitted fabric separating each double yarn-over is thinner in the bird's eye pattern. Also, bird's eye is worked on a base of garter stitch, like many of the original Shetland patterns, whereas cat's eye is worked on a base of stockinette.

Properties:
↔
The openwork mesh formed by this pattern is extremely elastic in all directions.

Yarn Consumption:
The allover pattern of double yarn-overs creates an openwork mesh, decreasing yarn consumption considerably.

Suggested Uses:
00–4

This pattern is traditionally used as a background stitch to offset more intricate lace pattern in shawls and stoles. To avoid a fabric with raised garter stitch ribs, work the pattern with very fine yarn.

Pattern:

(multiple of 4 stitches)

ROW 1 (WS): * K2tog, (yo) twice, k2tog; rep from *.

ROW 2: * K1, (k1, p1) into double yo of previous row, k1; rep from *.

ROW 3: K2, * k2tog, (yo) twice, k2tog; rep from * to last 2 sts, end k2.

ROW 4: K2, * k1, (k1, p1) into double yo of previous row, k1; rep from * to last 2 sts, end k2.

122.

PRINT O' THE WAVE

Other Name: Coral lace.

General Description:

This is one version of a traditional Shetland motif featuring waves. In it, the body of the wave is formed in stockinette and its foam crest with yarn-overs. The other version, used in the wave lace edging, uses yarn-overs to form the body of the wave, which is surrounded by stockinette.

Properties: The even-tensioned fabric has excellent drape.

Yarn Consumption:	The yarn-overs open up the fabric considerably, decreasing yarn consumption noticeably.

Suggested Uses: Perfect for a lace wrap, the pattern as given will produce waves that break to the left, though it can be reversed to create waves that break in the other direction. Experiment to create a unique version of this traditional motif.

Pattern: **(multiple of 16 stitches)**

ROW 1 (WS) AND ALL OTHER WRONG-SIDE ROWS: Purl.
ROW 2: * K2, (yo, k2tog) twice, (yo, k1) twice, k1, ssk, k3, k2tog; rep from *.
ROW 4: * K1, (yo, k2tog) twice, yo, k3, yo, k2, ssk, k1, k2tog, k1; rep from *.
ROW 6: * yo, k2tog, yo, ssk, yo, k5, yo, k2, k3tog, k2; rep from *.
ROW 8: * K1, (yo, ssk) twice, yo, k2, ssk, k3, k2tog, k2, yo; rep from *.
ROW 10: * K2, (yo, ssk) twice, yo, k2, ssk, k1, k2tog, k2, yo, k1; rep from *.
ROW 12: * K3, (yo, ssk) twice, yo, k2, k3tog, k2, yo, k2; rep from *.

123. **OBSTACLES**

General
Description:

This unusual pattern uses stacks of openwork Vs off-set with alternating backgrounds of stockinette and reverse stockinette to create a heavily three-dimensional pattern reminiscent of flowing ribbons. Because the yarn-overs are worked in the stockinette sections, they are purled on the wrong side.

Properties:
↔

The elastic fabric has a raised design, more like ribbing than traditional lacework, although it does block out nicely to show the interlocking eyelets. The wrong side is also compelling, with protruding orbs atop stockinette columns, like stacked mushrooms.

Yarn
Consumption:

Unlike most lace patterns, this stitch's alternating bands of stockinette and reverse stockinette draw in the fabric, increasing yarn consumption, unless heavily blocked.

Suggested Uses:
 00–12

With its interesting pattern and natural cushion, this pattern would make an excellent scarf when worked in a worsted-weight yarn. Also try it for the cuff of a sock—it has all the visual benefits of an interesting lace pattern along with the elasticity of a ribbing.

Pattern: **(multiple of 14 stitches)**

> **NOTE:** On wrong side, purl into yarn-overs from previous row.
>
> **ROW 1:** * P2, k2tog, k3, yo, k1, yo, k3, skp, p1; rep from *.
>
> **ROW 2 AND ALL OTHER WRONG-SIDE ROWS:** Knit the knit stitches and purl the purl stitches.
>
> **ROW 3:** * P2, k2tog, k2, yo, k3, yo, k2 skp, p1; rep from *.
>
> **ROW 5:** * P2, k2tog, k1, yo, k5, yo, k1, skp, p1; rep from *.
>
> **ROW 7:** * P2, k2tog, yo, k7, yo, skp, p1; rep from *.
>
> **ROW 9:** * K1, yo, k3, skp, p3, k2tog, k3, yo; rep from *.
>
> **ROW 11:** * K2, yo, k2, skp, p3, k2tog, k2, yo, k1; rep from *.
>
> **ROW 13:** * K3, yo, k1, skp, p3, k2tog, k1, yo, k2; rep from *.
>
> **ROW 15:** * K4, yo, skp, p3, k2tog, yo, k3; rep from *.
>
> **ROW 16:** See Row 2.

124. 📷

CATHERINE WHEELS

General Description: Let's assume this pattern of concentric circles is named for spinning fireworks and not a medieval torture device—both share the pattern's name and design.

Properties: This pattern groups a series of yarn-overs into a design on a bed of stockinette. The lightly textured fabric has good drape.

Yarn Consumption: The grouping of yarn-overs draws the fabric open, decreasing yarn consumption slightly if worked as an allover pattern.

Suggested Uses: This panel would be a fun insertion into the front of a child's cardigan. It could also be combined with other eyelet patterns to create a unique, openwork fabric for a sweater or wrap.

Pattern: **(panel of 13 stitches)**

WORK 5 TOG: With yarn in back, sl 3 sts purlwise, * pass 2nd st on RH needle over 1st (center) st, slip center st back to LH needle, pass 2nd st on LH needle over *, slip center st back to RH needle; rep from * to * once more, purl center st. (Note: Stitch referred to as "center" stitch is center one of 5 sts.)

ROW 1 (WS) AND ALL OTHER WRONG-SIDE ROWS: Purl.
ROW 2: K5, sl 3, yf, pass same slipped sts back to LH needle, yb, k3 slipped sts, k5.
ROW 4: K3, k3tog, yo, kf/b/f, yo, k3tog tbl, k3.
ROW 6: K1, k3tog, yo, k2tog, yo, kf/b/f, yo, skp, yo, k3tog tbl, k1.
ROW 8: (K2tog, yo) 3 times, k1 tbl, (yo, skp) 3 times.
ROW 10: K1, (yo, k2tog) twice, yo, sk2p, (yo, skp)

twice, yo, k1.

ROW 12: (Skp, yo) 3 times, k1-tbl, (yo, k2tog) 3 times.

ROW 14: K1, kf/b, yo, skp, yo, work 5 tog, yo, k2tog, yo, kf/b, k1.

ROW 16: K3, kf/b, yo, work 5 tog, yo, kf/b, k3.

---

125. 📷 **ROSE LEAF LACE**

Other Names: Double rose leaf.

General Description: This Victorian-era pattern is very similar to beech leaf lace; both are double leaf designs surrounded by yarn-overs. The difference lies in the shaping of the leaves: Rose leaf lace has wider but shorter leaves than its beech leaf cousin.

Properties: The stockinette leaves are surrounded entirely by yarn-overs, limiting the structure of the fabric. Consequently, it has excellent drape and some subtle texture due to the decreases on each leaf.

Yarn Consumption: Despite the stockinette leaves, the yarn-overs open up the fabric considerably, decreasing yarn consumption.

Suggested Uses: 0–6 This is another lace pattern that would be stunning as a border or edging on a shawl. Also consider knitting a single or double panel and sewing it onto the edge of a pillowcase or tablecloth to give linens a special touch.

Pattern: **(panel of 17 stitches)**

NOTE: Stitch count changes from row to row and is restored only in row 8.

ROW 1 (WS): Purl.

ROW 2: K1, yo, k1, ssk, p1, k2tog, k1, p1, k1, ssk, p1, k2tog, k1, yo, k1.

ROW 3: P4, (k1, p2) twice, k1, p4.

ROW 4: (K1, yo) twice, ssk, p1, k2tog, p1, ssk, p1, k2tog, (yo, k1) twice.

ROW 5: P5, (k1, p1) twice, k1, p5.

ROW 6: K1, yo, k3, yo, sk2p, p1, k3tog, yo, k3, yo, k1.

ROW 7: P7, k1, p7.

ROW 8: K1, yo, k5, yo, sk2p, yo, k5, yo, k1.

126. 📷 **APPLE LEAF LACE**

General Description: This pattern of rounded leaves staggered on a bed of garter stitch was re-created from pictures of early nineteenth-century lace. Once worked, its simple construction is evident. The pattern can be easily reworked to form a single panel or an edging.

Properties: The embossed, lightly textured fabric has a bias, which will cause the horizontal edges to wave in and out with each row repeat.

Yarn
Consumption:

The bed of reverse stockinette draws in the fabric and counteracts any opening effect of the eyelets, causing this pattern to use approximately the same amount of yarn as stockinette.

Suggested Uses:

\ 0–6

As a pretty lace design with substantial coverage, consider this stitch for a child's cardigan or a heavier wrap or stole.

Pattern:

(multiple of 18 stitches + 1)

ROW 1 (WS) AND ALL OTHER WRONG-SIDE ROWS: Purl.
ROW 2: * K4, k2tog, p2, (k1, yo) twice, k1, p2, ssk, k3; rep from *, end k1.
ROW 4: * K3, k2tog, p2, k2, (yo, k1) twice, k1, p2, ssk, k2; rep from *, end k1.
ROW 6: * K2, k2tog, p2, k3, (yo, k1) twice, k2, p2, ssk, k1; rep from *, end k1.
ROW 8: * K1, k2tog, p2, k4, (yo, k1) twice, k3, p2, ssk; rep from *, end k1.
ROW 10: * K1, yo, k1, p2, ssk, k7, k2tog, p2, k1, yo; rep from *, end k1.
ROW 12: * K1, yo, k2, p2, ssk, k5, k2tog, p2, k2, yo; rep from *, end k1.
ROW 14: * K1, yo, k3, p2, ssk, k3, k2tog, p2, k3, yo; rep from *, end k1.
ROW 16: * K1, yo, k4, p2, ssk, k1, k2tog, p2, k4, yo; rep from *, end k1.

127. 📷 **FLEMISH DIAMONDS**

Other Name: Flemish block lace.

General
Description: This pattern's name is misleading on all counts. The shapes are rectangles, not diamonds, although that part of the name comes from its relation to the basic openwork diamonds stitch pattern. Though the pattern is also named after the famed Flemish brickwork, a bricklayer would call this pattern's block arrangement herringbone—the Flemish brick arrangement is something completely different.

Properties: The crisp lines of yarn-overs give the fabric excellent drape, despite the surrounding bricks solid of stockinette. The fabric will not have a bias, as its increases and decreases are evenly matched.

Yarn
Consumption: The continuous lines of yarn-overs open up the fabric, decreasing yarn consumption noticeably.

🧵🧵

Suggested Uses: A handsome geometric pattern, it would do nicely as
╲ 0–6 the center motif in a long stole, paired perhaps with Madeira fans or swinging triangles to accentuate its straight lines and bold pattern.

Pattern: **(multiple of 14 stitches + 3)**

ROW 1 (WS) AND ALL OTHER WRONG-SIDE ROWS: Purl.

ROW 2: K2, * k2tog, yo, k1, yo, ssk, k3, k2tog, yo, k4; rep from *, end k1.

ROW 4: K1, * k2tog, yo, k3, yo, ssk, k1, k2tog, yo, k4; rep from *, end k2.

ROW 6: K2tog, yo, * k5, yo, sk2p, yo, k4, k2tog, yo; rep from *, end k1.

ROW 8: K2, * yo, ssk, k4, yo, ssk, k3, k2tog, yo, k1; rep from *, end k1.

ROW 10: K3, * yo, ssk, k4, yo, ssk, k1, k2tog, yo, k3; rep from *.

ROW 12: K4, * yo, ssk, k4, yo, k3tog, yo, k5; rep from *, end last repeat k4.

128a–b.

ARROWHEAD LACE

Other Name: Small lace chevron.

General Description: This looks like zigzag trellis on its side, which is essentially true: In the zigzag trellis pattern, left- and right-biased faggot stitches are stacked atop each other, whereas here they are placed side by side to create a series of stacked arrowheads, or reverse chevrons.

Properties: The mesh fabric has both excellent drape and elasticity. It has no bias, as its increases and decreases are evenly matched.

Yarn
Consumption:

The stacked rows of yarn-overs open up the fabric considerably, decreasing yarn consumption substantially.

Suggested Uses:

0–6

With a strong vertical axis and diagonal lines, this pattern would make a flattering summer top. The fabric's mesh properties would also make it a practical choice for a fun beach bag—just shake to get the sand out.

Pattern:

(multiple of 10 stitches + 1)

ROWS 1 AND 3 (WS): Purl.
ROW 2: K1, * (yo, ssk) twice, k1, (k2tog, yo) twice, k1; rep from *.
ROW 4: K2, * yo, ssk, yo, sk2p, yo, k2tog, yo, k3; rep from *, end last repeat k2.

Variation:

Little Arrowhead Lace (multiple of 6 stitches + 1)
When the "twice" is removed from the arrowhead lace instructions, a miniature arrowhead pattern emerges; however, without defined diagonal lines, this design looks more like creeping spiders on a string.

ROWS 1 AND 3 (WS): Purl.
ROW 2: K1, * yo, ssk, k1, k2tog, yo, k1; rep from *.
ROW 4: K2, * yo, sk2p, yo, k3; rep from *, end last repeat k2.

129. 📷 **CANDELABRA PANEL**

Other Name: Eyelet fans.

General
Description:
Rows of eyelets travel outward from a central "candle-stick" of knit stitches. This is not an elaborate candle pattern like candlelight lace or flickering flames but rather a simple eyelet pattern named for its appearance of outstretched arms.

Properties: The open, lightly textured fabric has no bias. The candelabra arms are placed on a bed of stockinette.

Yarn
Consumption:
The rows of eyelets open up the fabric, decreasing yarn consumption.

Suggested Uses: This simple eyelet panel would be a nice accent on any stockinette project, whether a bag, sweater, or hat; used sparingly, it should not decrease a garment's warmth noticeably. Reworked upside down and over one row repeat, it would add an interesting accent to the bottom hem of a blouse.

Pattern: **(panel of 13 stitches)**

ROW 1: Knit.
ROW 2 AND ALL OTHER WRONG-SIDE ROWS: Purl.
ROW 3: Knit.
ROW 5: K4, k2tog, yo, k1, yo, skp, k4.

ROW 7: K3, k2tog, yo, k3, yo, skp, k3.

ROW 9: K2, (k2tog, yo) twice, k1, (yo, skp) twice, k2.

ROW 11: K1, (k2tog, yo) twice, k3, (yo, skp) twice, k1.

ROW 13: (K2tog, yo) 3 times, k1, (yo, skp) 3 times.

ROW 14: Purl.

130.

HAREBELL LACE

General Description:

Named for the delicate, bell-shaped wildflower found in the grasslands of Scotland, this simple lace pattern forms the shape of its namesake with graceful ease.

Properties:

Small stockinette flowers are outlined by purl stitches and surrounded by yarn-overs, creating a fabric with excellent drape and a bit of depth, as well.

Yarn Consumption:

The background of yarn-overs opens up the fabric considerably, decreasing yarn consumption noticeably.

Suggested Uses:

0–6

This classic lace pattern would make a charming summer cardigan or a precious baby blanket. It would also make a pretty scarf for the early months of spring, when heavy woolens are no longer needed but there is still a chill in the air.

Pattern:

(multiple of 6 stitches + 3)

ROWS 1, 3, AND 5 (WS): P3, * k3, p3; rep from *.

ROW 2: K3, * p2tog, yo, p1, k3; rep from *.
ROW 4: K3, * p1, yo, p2tog, k3; rep from *.
ROW 6: K1, k2tog, * (p1, yo) twice, p1, sk2p; rep from
  *, end last repeat ssk, k1.
ROWS 7, 9, AND 11: K3, * p3, k3; rep from *.
ROW 8: P1, yo, p2tog, * k3, p1, yo, p2tog; rep from *.
ROW 10: P2tog, yo, p1, * k3, p2tog, yo, p1; rep from *.
ROW 12: P2, yo, p1, * sk2p, (p1, yo) twice, p1, rep
  from *, end sk2p, p1, yo, p2.

131. **GRAND TREFOIL**

General
Description:

Named for its clusters of three grand eyelets—eyelets
formed by dropping the second loop of a double
yarn-over—this simple pattern creates a beautiful and
intricate mesh.

Properties:

This pattern creates a reversible fabric—an unusual
characteristic in lace—and the allover grand eyelets
design lends extreme vertical and horizontal stretch as
well as excellent drape. Because of this, cast on and
bind off very loosely; it is also helpful to leave both
loops of the double yarn-over on the needle and bind
off each loop separately.

Yarn
Consumption:

As a web of double-sized holes, the fabric is extremely
open and uses significantly less yarn than stockinette.

Suggested Uses: By itself, this pattern would make a striking stole or
0–6 scarf; coupling it with a well-chosen border and edging could make an heirloom piece. Note that its
extreme stretch might cause complications if joined to
less elastic stockinette-based eyelet patterns.

Pattern: **(multiple of 5 stitches + 3)**

DL: Drop the second loop of the double yo of previous
row off the needle—the first loop is already knitted.

ROW 1 (PREPARATION): K3, * (yo) twice, k2tog, k3;
rep from *.
ROW 2: K5, * DL, (yo) twice, k2tog, k3; rep from *,
end last repeat k1.
ROW 3: K3, * DL, k2, (yo) twice, k2tog, k1; rep from *.
ROW 4: K3, * DL, (yo) twice, k2tog, k3; rep from *.
Repeat Rows 1–3.

132. **STARLIGHT LACE**

General This elegant openwork pattern uses double decreases
Description: to expand the stars at their central points, causing the
stitch count to change from row to row.

Properties: This pattern creates a mesh of diamond stars with
 greatly increased lateral and horizontal stretch and
excellent drape.

Yarn
Consumption:

The extensive use of yarn-overs opens the fabric considerably, decreasing yarn consumption significantly.

Suggested Uses:

\ 00–4

This stitch would be a delicate and stunning allover pattern for any lace project. Try it as the central motif in a stole, bordered with gracenote lace.

Pattern:

⚠

(multiple of 6 stitches + 5)

NOTE: The stitch count changes from row to row. Original count is restored in Rows 8 and 16.

ROW 1 (WS) AND ALL OTHER WRONG-SIDE ROWS: Purl.

ROW 2: K2, * yo, ssk, k1, yo, ssk, k1 tbl; rep from *, end yo, ssk, k1.

ROW 4: K3, * k2tog, yo, k1 tbl, yo, ssk, k1 tbl; rep from *, end k2.

ROW 6: K2, k2tog, * yo, s2kp, yo, sk2p; rep from *, end yo, s2kp, yo, ssk, k2.

ROW 8: K3, * k1 tbl, yo, k1, yo, k1 tbl, k1; rep from *, end k2.

ROW 10: K2, * yo, ssk, k1 tbl, yo, ssk, k1; rep from *, end yo, ssk, k1.

ROW 12: * K2tog, yo, k1 tbl, yo, ssk, k1 tbl; rep from *, end k2tog, yo, k1 tbl, yo, ssk.

ROW 14: K1, * yo, s2kp, yo, sk2p; rep from *, end yo, s2kp, yo, k1.

ROW 16: K1, k1tbl, * k1, yo, k1 tbl, k1, k1 tbl, yo; rep from *, end k1, k1 tbl, k1.

133. **ROSEBUD MESH**

General
Description:

This busy pattern draws the eye in all directions as a web of openwork rosebuds stretch across the fabric to create a lace mesh.

Properties:

This pattern's vertical lines of rosebuds and triangle leaves give the mesh a bit more substance and structure than basic mesh fabrics. But true to form, the majority of the fabric is open and has excellent drape.

Yarn
Consumption:

The extensive use of yarn-overs opens the fabric considerably, decreasing yarn consumption substantially.

Suggested Uses:

00–4

The spreading bud and leaf design makes this stitch excellent as an allover pattern to cover large areas in any lace project. Consider pairing it with a leaf-based border or panel insertion to extend the botanical theme.

Pattern:

(multiple of 10 stitches + 1)

ROW 1 (WS) AND ALL OTHER WRONG-SIDE ROWS: Purl.
ROW 2: K2tog, * yo, k3, yo, kf/b, yo, k3, yo, sk2p;
rep from *, end last repeat ssk instead of sk2p.
ROW 4: Ssk, * yo, s2kp, yo, k2tog, yo, ssk, (yo, s2kp)
twice; rep from *, end last repeat k2tog instead of
the second s2kp.
ROW 6: K2, * k2tog, yo, k3, yo, ssk, k3; rep from *,
end last repeat k2.

ROW 8: K1, * k2tog, yo, k1 tbl, yo, sk2p, yo, k1 tbl, yo, ssk, k1; rep from *.

134. **GRACENOTE**

General Description:

In musical notation, a grace note represents a quick accent note played just an instant before a more substantial note. Its written symbol, a small staff and flag with a diagonal strikethrough, is somewhat reminiscent of this lace panel's climbing staffs and flags.

Properties:

With characteristics similar to braided eyelets, this pattern forms a fabric with strips of eyelets separated by solid blocks of stockinette. The stockinette areas anchor the fabric and give it some substance, while the eyelet strips significantly increase drape.

Yarn Consumption:

The climbing lines of yarn-overs open the fabric, decreasing yarn consumption noticeably.

Suggested Uses:

00–4

This pattern would serve as an interesting border for other eyelet lace patterns, such as Flemish block lace. Also try working it as a multiple of 15 stitches rather than as a panel—the flags on either side will fit nicely into the nook on the other side and create a zigzag border of stockinette between each repeat.

Pattern: **(panel of 15 stitches)**

ROW 1 (WS) AND ALL OTHER WRONG-SIDE ROWS: Purl.
ROW 2: K4, k2tog, yo, k2, k2tog, yo, k3, yo, ssk.
ROW 4: K3, k2tog, yo, (k1, yo, ssk) twice, k1, k2tog, yo, k1.
ROW 6: K2, k2tog, yo, k3, yo, ssk, k1, yo, k3tog, yo, k2.
ROW 8: K1, k2tog, yo, k1, yo, ssk, k2, yo, ssk, k2tog, yo, k3.
ROW 10: K2tog, yo, k3, yo, ssk, k2, yo, ssk, k4.
ROW 12: K1, yo, ssk, (k1, k2tog, yo) twice, k1, yo, ssk, k3.
ROW 14: K2, yo, sk2p, yo, k1, k2tog, yo, k3, yo, ssk, k2.
ROW 16: K3, yo, ssk, k2tog, yo, k2, k2tog, yo, k1, yo, ssk, k1.

---

135. 📷 **VEINED LEAF PANEL**

General
Description:

This panel pattern forms a design of leaves stacked along a vertically aligned axis, and the wide-based eyelet centers taper in width as they rise into each leaf.

Properties:
↔

This pattern forms a narrow, embossed panel of stockinette on reverse stockinette. The strip of double eyelets in the center of each leaf open up the solid fabric, giving it increased drape and stretch.

Yarn
Consumption:
🧵🧵

The eyelets draw out the fabric, particularly on the lateral axis, decreasing yarn consumption.

Suggested Uses:

00–4

This pattern would be suitable as a border for any lace or eyelet pattern of substance—its larger areas of stockinette would overpower a lighter lace or mesh such as falling leaves or rosebud mesh.

Pattern:

(panel of 9 stitches)

NOTE: Stitch count changes from row to row. Original count is restored in Rows 9–12.

ROW 1: P3, (k1, yo) twice, k1, p3.
ROW 2: K3, p5, k3.
ROW 3: P3, k2, yo, k1, yo, k2, p3.
ROW 4: K3, p7, k3.
ROW 5: P3, ssk, k1, (yo, k1) twice, k2tog, p3.
ROW 6: Repeat Row 4.
ROW 7: P3, ssk, k3, k2tog, p3.
ROW 8: Repeat Row 2.
ROW 9: P3, ssk, k1, k2tog, p3.
ROW 10: K3, p3, k3.
ROW 11: P3, yo, s2kp, yfrn, p3.
ROW 12: Repeat Row 10.

136a–d.

ORENBURG LACE

General Description:

The traditional knitted shawls particular to Orenburg, a Russian fortress town at the base of the Ural Mountains on the border with Kazakhstan, give this

form of lace its name. These shawls are renowned for
their intricate patterns worked in the finest cashmere,
which comes from the down combed from the under-
belly of a special breed of goat unique to the region.
The shawls are traditionally about six feet (2 m)
square and are so fine that they can be easily slipped
through a wedding ring. A gift of one of these prized
pieces to Queen Victoria is thought to have influ-
enced her encouragement of lace shawl knitting in the
United Kingdom, resulting in the explosion of the
Shetland shawl industry during her reign.

Properties: Orenburg lace uses garter stitch as its base, and in
support of the connection with Shetland knitting, the
earliest Shetland shawls were also based on garter
stitch. The Shetland pattern evolved to use a stockinette base as well, while Orenburg lace retained the
exclusive use of garter stitch. The wonder of Orenburg
lace is that these amazingly intricate pieces are formed
by ten extremely basic stitch patterns—four of which
are presented here—so simple in their construction
that there was no need for the peasant women who
created these masterpieces to do any but the most
basic charting of a shawl's design before embarking on
its creation (which can take up to 270 hours for an
expert Orenburg knitter from the region to complete). Only three stitches are used in Orenburg
lace—the knit stitch, the yarn-over, and the knit-
2or3-together—yet these very basic building blocks

are combined to create intricate pieces of gossamer fabric, lighter than dandelion seeds blowing in the wind yet warm enough to keep the nomadic Tartars and Cossacks of the Eurasian steppes warm during their cruel, wind-blown winters.

Yarn Consumption:

The use of yarn-overs opens up the fabric considerably, but yarn consumption will depend mostly on how the small building blocks are arranged and how large the swaths of garter stitch within each motif are.

Suggested Uses:

00–4

As written, these patterns will create vertically stacked openwork patterns. Chart them and combine them with each other to create an Orenburg-inspired shawl or lace project. To achieve the same gossamer effect found in traditional Orenburg lace, select the finest cobweb-weight cashmere.

Patterns:

Strawberry (multiple of 9 stitches)

The most popular basic stitch pattern of Orenburg lace, six cobweb yarn-overs are arranged in a circle to create a round strawberry similar to the basic flower eyelet lace pattern. It is commonly used in all sections of Orenburg shawls but is often found—singularly or combined with itself to create a more intricate pattern—in the center of diamond motifs.

ROW 1: * K3, (yo, k2tog) twice, k2; rep from *.
ROW 2 AND ALL OTHER WRONG-SIDE ROWS: Knit.
ROW 3: * K1, k2tog, yo, k3, yo, k2tog, k1; rep from *.
ROW 5: * K3, yo, k3tog, yo, k3; rep from *
ROW 6: See Row 2.

Fish Eye (multiple of 4 stitches)

This configuration of three yarn-overs is worked on both the right-side and wrong-side rows, and its basic element is reminiscent of that in grand trefoil lace. Its stack of yarn-overs lends it to the creation of larger horizontal, lateral, diagonal, and cross designs.

ROWS 1, 2, AND 3: * K2, yo, k2tog; rep from *.
ROW 4: Knit.

Blinov, Honeycomb, or *Samovar* (multiple of 6 stitches + 2)

Named for its creator, Blinova, this pattern is simple in appearance and brilliant for the way its extremely basic elements combine to create an elaborate design of crisscrossing diagonals of yarn-overs and decreases. Like the strawberry, it is generally found in all sections of Orenburg shawls.

ROWS 1 AND 2: K1, * k2, yo, k2tog, k2; rep from *, end k1.

ROWS 3 AND 4: K1, * yo, k2tog, k2, yo, k2tog; rep
from *, end k1.

ROWS 5 AND 6: Repeat Rows 1 and 2.

Repeat Rows 3–6.

Mouseprint (multiple of 6 stitches)

Similar to the simple eyelet diamond pattern, the
mouseprint is a four-hole diamond worked on the
right-side rows. It is traditionally used in borders and
to fill the space around the central motif of the shawl.

ROW 1: * K2, yo, k2tog, k2; rep from *.

ROW 2 AND ALL OTHER WRONG-SIDE ROWS: Knit.

ROW 3: * K1, (yo, k2tog) twice, k1; rep from *.

ROW 5: Repeat Row 1.

ROW 6: See Row 2.

Ribbings and Edgings

PLAIN RIBBING

137a–e.

General
Description:

Ribbing patterns use the natural offsetting tension of knit and purl stitches to create a fabric that pulls in on itself. Plain ribbing alternates strips of stockinette and reverse stockinette of varying widths—(k1, p1), (k4, p2), for example—and examples can be found on the cuffs of most machine-knit sweaters.

Properties:

Plain ribbing creates an even-tensioned fabric that is reversible when the pattern calls for an equal number of stitches in each vertical strip. Left alone, the lateral spread will be narrower than stockinette, although the lateral stretch is greater than stockinette—that is, when pulled from its sides, the fabric will stretch further than a piece of stockinette with the same amount of stitches. The fabric is also slightly thicker than stockinette because the bands overlap when the fabric is at rest.

Yarn
Consumption:

The offsetting tension of the knit and purl bands draw the fabric in on itself, so plain ribbing uses noticeably more yarn than stockinette.

Suggested Uses:
00–12+

Plain ribbing could be used wherever elasticity is desired, such as around the hem or cuffs of a sweater, along the edge of a hat or mittens, or at the tops of socks. Because the fabric is thicker than stockinette, consider knitting ribbed edges with a needle two sizes smaller than that used for the main piece of the project, or use fewer stitches for the ribbing and increase in the first row after the ribbing ends to the number required for the main piece.

Pattern:

2x2 Ribbing (multiple of 4 stitches)

ALL ROWS: * K2, p2; rep from *.

Variations:

1x1 Ribbing (even number of stitches)
The lowest common denominator of ribbing, this pattern will create a delicate ribbing with less elasticity than the commonly used k2, p2 ribbing.

ALL ROWS: * K1, p1; rep from *.

3x3 Ribbing (multiple of 6 stitches + 3)
This pattern will create slightly wider bands, making it good for projects with a little more bulk to them.

ROW 1: * K3, p3; rep from *, end k3.
ROW 2: * P3, k3; rep from *, end p3.

4x2 Ribbing (multiple of 6 stitches + 4)
This pattern is good if wide knit bands are desired. By making the purl bands only two stitches wide, their bumpy surface will not show when the fabric is at rest.

ROW 1: * K4, p2; rep from *, end k4.
ROW 2: P4, * k2, p4; rep from *.

5x1 Ribbing or *Knife Pleats* (multiple of 6 stitches + 5)
This pattern is more popular for its appearance than its elasticity. The strips of single purl stitches create thin vertical lines down the front of the fabric for a mock pleating look.

ROW 1: * K5, p1; rep from *, end k5.
ROW 2: P5, * k1, p5; rep from *.

138a-b. 📷

DIAGONAL RIBBING

General
Description:

Similar to the technique used to create mock cables, this clever pattern uses slipped stitches and twisted stitches to create a right-leaning ribbing.

Properties:
↔

The deep, fluffy ribs reduce the thick, dense fabric's drape significantly. Although the fabric is not reversible, the wrong side is also attractive—its slip-stitch bars create a broken diagonal pattern.

Yarn
Consumption:

Suggested Uses:

\ 00–12+

The deep ribs pull in the fabric, increasing yarn consumption noticeably.

The thickness and practically nonexistent drape suits this fabric to heavy winter garments, such as sturdy sweaters or jackets. Its structured appearance makes it tempting for a knitted bag, but use a fabric lining or other additional reinforcement to combat the pattern's multidirectional elasticity.

Pattern:

TW2: Skip 1 st and knit into the back loop of 2nd st, then knit the skipped st through the front loop, then drop both sts from needle together.

Diagonal Ribbing R **(multiple of 3 stitches)**

ROW 1 (WS): K2, * sl 1 wyif, k2; rep from *, end k1.
ROW 2: K1, p2, * TW2, p1; rep from *, end last repeat, k1.
ROW 3: K1, * sl 1 wyif, k2; rep from *, end last repeat, k1.
ROW 4: K1, * TW2, p1; rep from *, end k2.
ROW 5: K1, * k2, sl 1 wyif; rep from *, end k2.
ROW 6: K1, * p1, TW2; rep from *, end last repeat k1 instead of TW2.

Variation:

Diagonal Ribbing L (multiple of 8 stitches + 6)
This simpler version of diagonal ribbing is a standard 4x4 ribbing, shifted one stitch to the left on each subsequent row to create a left-leaning rib. To create a

right-leaning rib, either work the pattern backward
from Row 8 to Row 1 or use the wrong side of the
pattern as given.

ROW 1: P2, * k4, p4; rep from *, end k4.
ROW 2: P3, * k4, p4; rep from *, end k3.
ROW 3: P4, * k4, p4; rep from *, end k2.
ROW 4: P1, * k4, p4; rep from *, end k4, p1.
ROW 5: K2, * p4, k4; rep from *, end p4.
ROW 6: K3, * p4, k4; rep from *, end p3.
ROW 7: K4, * p4, k4; rep from *, end p2.
ROW 8: K1, * p4, k4; rep from *, end p4, k1.

139a–b.

BROKEN RIB

General
Description:

This pattern could just as easily be considered a
knit/purl check pattern—it lacks the elasticity of ribbing and is only called such because rows three and
four are worked (k2, p2). Experimenting with the
width of each rib strip—changing (k2, p2) to (k4, p2)
for example—and the number of rows over which the
ribbing and stockinette background is worked will
drastically alter the characteristic of the broken rib
pattern, and it is well worth the time. When broken
rib is worked in its smallest possible variation—(k1,
p1) every other row on a field of stockinette—it is
also known as rice stitch.

Properties:	The textured fabric has a geometric design and less elasticity than plain ribbing. Though not reversible, the wrong side is also attractive.
Yarn Consumption:	Because the ribbing is broken by bands of stockinette, the fabric does not draw in on itself significantly. This pattern will use approximately the same amount of yarn as stockinette.
Suggested Uses:	This pattern could replace stockinette whenever a subtle geometric pattern is desired over a field of plain fabric.

Pattern: **(multiple of 4 stitches + 2)**

ROW 1 (WS): Purl.
ROW 2: Knit.
ROW 3: K2, * p2, k2; rep from *.
ROW 4: P2, * k2, p2; rep from *.

Variation: *Stairstep Rib* or *Broken Diagonal* (multiple of 8 stitches)
This pattern is (k4, p4) ribbing "shifted" so that every four rows the vertical alignment of the ribbing strips moves two stitches to the right. To shift the strips to the left, work the pattern backward from Row 16 to Row 1.

ROWS 1, 2, 3, AND 4: * P4, k4; rep from *.
ROWS 5 AND 7: K2, * p4, k4; rep from *, end last repeat k2.

ROWS 6 AND 8: P2, * k4, p4; rep from *, end last
repeat p2.

ROWS 9, 10, 11, AND 12: * K4, p4; rep from *.

ROWS 13 AND 15: P2, * k4, p4; rep from *, end last
repeat p2.

ROWS 14 AND 16: K2, * p4, k4; rep from *, end last
repeat k2.

---

140. 📷 **EMBOSSED MOSS STITCH RIB**

General
Description:
This attractive pattern forms fancy textured columns
bordered by crisp vertical strips of knit stitches.

Properties:
The raised, textured fabric has elasticity similar to its
base stitch, 4x3 ribbing. The fabric—its columns of
moss stitches particularly—is thicker than stockinette.

Yarn
Consumption:
The uneven tension of the knit and purl vertical strips
pulls the fabric in on itself, noticeably increasing yarn
consumption.

Suggested Uses:
00–8
Consider this pattern for any project needing strong
vertical lines. It would add a touch of interest to the
edge bands of any sweater and would be a nice choice
for an allover ribbing pattern or as edging along the
front of a cardigan. Unlike diagonal ribbing, it has
some vertical structure and would be suitable for a
knitted bag.

Pattern: **(multiple of 7 stitches + 3)**

ROW 1: P3, * k1, p1, k2, p3; rep from *.
ROW 2: K3, * p2, k1, p1, k3; rep from *.
ROW 3: P3, * K2, p1, k1, p3; rep from *.
ROW 4: K3, * p1, k1, p2, k3; rep from *.

---

141. **MISTAKE RIB**

General
Description:

Though constructed differently, this ribbing, with its lines of raised knit stitches, bears some resemblance to brioche stitch. Accidentally casting on one less stitch than needed for plain 2x2 ribbing is the "mistake" that gives this pattern its name.

Properties:
◯↔

The thick, reversible fabric has deep, textured ribs and elasticity comparable to plain ribbing.

Yarn
Consumption:

The ribbings draw in the fabric, increasing yarn consumption noticeably.

Suggested Uses:
\ 00–10

Mistake rib is popular as an unfussy scarf pattern. It's simple to work, has an interesting texture, and creates a warm, thick fabric perfect for wrapping around one's neck on a cold winter's day.

Pattern: **(multiple of 4 stitches + 3)**

ALL ROWS: * K2, p2; rep from *, end k2, p1.

---

142. 📷 **FISHERMAN'S RIB**

General
Description:
Fishermen quite likely enjoyed this stitch for the double-thick fabric it created—knitting into the stitch below creates a double loop around the new stitch, giving this fabric increased depth and warmth.

Properties:
○ ↔
The thick, reversible fabric has deep, fluffy ribs and elasticity comparable to plain ribbing.

Yarn
Consumption:
With the double loops and deep ribbing, this pattern uses significantly more yarn than stockinette.

Suggested Uses:
00–10
This pattern would make a deliciously warm scarf—with some fringe added to the end, it would be a handsome and appreciated addition to anyone's cold-weather wardrobe. The stitch would also be attractive as an allover pattern for a heavy sweater.

Pattern:
(multiple of 2 stitches)

PREPARATION ROW (WS): Purl.
ALL SUBSEQUENT ROWS: * P1, knit next st in the row
    below; rep from *, p2.

143. **SLIP-STITCH RIBBING**

General
Description:

This pattern uses the pronounced effect of slip stitches to create rounded columns bordered by crisp vertical strips of knit stitches—a contrast to the flat, textured columns of embossed moss stitch rib.

Properties:

The raised, textured fabric is thicker than stockinette and has elasticity similar to its base stitch, 3x2 ribbing.

Yarn
Consumption:

The uneven tension of the knit and purl vertical strips causes the fabric to pull in on itself, increasing yarn consumption noticeably.

Suggested Uses:

00–8

Though this pattern is a subtle yet interesting substitute for plain ribbing in almost any application, its rounded columns would also make perfect tree trunks. Try knitting one column on a field of reverse stockinette and twisting stitches to branch off the three strips of knit stitches at the top. Create "leaves" with small bobbles or popcorn stitch.

Pattern:

(multiple of 5 stitches + 2)

ROW 1 (WS): K2, * p3, k2; rep from *.
ROW 2: P2, * k1, sl 1 wyib, k1, p2; rep from *.

144.   **FAGGOTING RIB**

Other Name:

Half herringbone.

General
Description:

While ribbing is generally associated with thick,
dense fabrics, this pattern is quite the contrary:
It uses faggoting instead of purl stitches as the foil
to its strong vertical strips, creating a lace-based
ribbing.

Properties:

↔

This delicate pattern alternates single-stitch strips of
garter stitch with strips of faggoting to create a ribbed
mesh with excellent lateral stretch and significantly
increased drape compared to plain ribbing.

Yarn
Consumption:

The faggoting base opens up the fabric considerably,
decreasing yarn consumption noticeably.

Suggested Uses:

\ 00–8

This pattern would be a nice edging for a lace
blouse—its strong vertical lines bring to mind traditional ribbing, but without the added bulk.

Pattern:

(multiple of 3 stitches)

ALL ROWS: * K1, yo, k2tog; rep from *.

145a–d. **CABLE RIBBING**

General
Description:

By knitting the cable stitches through the back loops, in the manner of the eastern knitting tradition, the "seat" of each stitch is twisted, giving the cables a lightly textured front and a touch of elegance.

Properties:

Though this is ostensibly a ribbing pattern, the cables reduce the fabric's elasticity. The thicker fabric and reduced drape, however, are similar to plain ribbing.

Yarn
Consumption:

Both the ribbing and the cable crossings draw in the fabric, increasing yarn consumption noticeably.

Suggested Uses:

00–8

This pattern's subtle details and delicate cables would make it a fine edging for a fancy sweater. Consider also knitting 3x2 ribbed socks and substituting this pattern for one of the knit panels along each side to dress them up.

Patterns:

Cable Ribbing L (multiple of 5 stitches + 2)

ROWS 1 AND 3 (WS): K2, * p1 tbl, k1, p1 tbl, k2; rep from *.
ROW 2: P2, * k1 tbl, p1, k1 tbl, p2; rep from *.
ROW 4: P2, * sl 2 sts to cn and hold in front, k1 tbl, then sl the purl st back to LH needle and purl it; then k1 tbl from cn; p2; rep from *.

Cable Ribbing R (multiple of 5 stitches + 2)

ROWS 1 AND 3 (WS): K2, * p1 tbl, k1, p1 tbl, k2; rep from *.

ROW 2: P2, * k1 tbl, p1, k1 tbl, p2; rep from *.

ROW 4: P2, * sl next 2 sts to cn and hold in back, k1 tbl, then sl the purl st back to LH needle and purl it; then k1 tbl from cn; p2; rep from *.

Variations: *Cable and Eyelet Ribbing* or *Picot Eyelet Cable*
This pattern is a longer and wider version of the cable ribbing, with eyelets inserted between each cable crossing.

Cable and Eyelet Ribbing L (panel of 10 stitches)
ROW 1 (WS): K2, p6, k2.
ROW 2: P2, k1, k2tog, (yo) twice, ssk, k1, p2.
ROW 3: K2, p2, (k1, p1) into the double yo of previous row, p2, k2.
ROW 4: P2, k6, p2.
ROW 5: Repeat Row 1.
ROW 6: P2, sl 4 sts to cn and hold in front, k2, then sl the center 2 sts from cn back to LH needle and knit them, then k2 from cn; p2.
ROWS 7–18: Repeat Rows 1–4, 3 times more.

Cable and Eyelet Ribbing R (panel of 10 stitches)
ROW 1 (WS): K2, p6, k2.
ROW 2: P2, k1, k2tog, (yo) twice, ssk, k1, p2.

ROW 3: K2, p2, (k1, p1) into the double yo of previous row, p2, k2.

ROW 4: P2, k6, p2.

ROW 5: Repeat Row 1.

ROW 6: P2, sl 4 sts to cn and hold in back, k2, then sl the center 2 sts from cn back to LH needle and knit them, then k2 from cn; p2.

ROWS 7–18: Repeat Rows 1–4, 3 times more.

146. **PLAIN HEM**

General Description:
This is the knitting version of the hem in sewn garments. Fabric is knit to the depth desired for the hem, a turning row is worked, and then the hem is folded up into the wrong side of the garment and stitched into place. For those who dislike seaming, instructions are given to avoid this last step—a simple and clever method of working the provisional edge stitches together with the stitches in the working round equidistant from the turning round.

Properties:
This technique creates a fabric that lies flat, with a straight edge. It will be thicker than the main portion of the project because the fabric is folded in on itself. To reduce the bulk, either work Rows 1–4 with a needle one or two sizes smaller or work fewer stitches in Rows 1–3 and increase to the required number of stitches in Row 4.

Yarn
Consumption:

This edge treatment can be worked in many stitch patterns, which will determine yarn consumption.

Suggested Uses:
\ 00–12+

This edge is suitable for any project that does not require an elastic edge and for which a flat, plain edge is desirable. It is a popular alternative to ribbing at the cuffs and edge of a sweater, and it can be used to knit a hat that will sit nicely upon one's head without wreaking havoc upon one's hair.

Instructions:

Cast on required number of stitches using a provisional cast-on method.

ROWS 1, 3, AND 5: Knit.

ROWS 2, 4, AND 6: Purl.

ROW 7 (TURNING ROW/FOLD LINE): Purl.

ROWS 8, 10, AND 12: Purl.

ROWS 9, 11, AND 13: Knit.

ROW 14: Unravel provisional cast-on and place free loops on a spare needle, pointing in same direction as last needle worked. Fold and work together 1 st from each needle.

147a–c.

PICOT EDGING

General
Description:

The word *picot* derives from the French verb *piquer*, which means "to prick"— in knitting, picot is a thin, looped or pointed edge, like the points on a crown.

Properties: These patterns form a pucker along the edge of the fabric. The cast-on and bind-off techniques produce a fabric that will not lie flat, which can be used to the project's advantage. By contrast, the picot hem lays flat, but its edge is a series of delicate points.

Yarn Consumption: As an edge treatment, this pattern requires only marginally more yarn than a standard cast-on, bind-off, or plain hem.

Suggested Uses: Picot edgings give projects a dainty flair. They are a nice alternative to ribbings in almost any application in which elasticity is not a main concern. Picot cast-on produces a puckered mock ruffle, which would be particularly suited to a spring or fall hat for a baby. Use the similar picot bind-off technique at the end of the project. Picot hem is a decorative and popular substitute for ribbing at the top edge of socks; the edge lies flat but has delicate points. To create a nicked edge rather than a pointed edge, insert knit stitches between each (yo, k2tog).

Instructions: **_Picot Cast-On_**

USING KNITTED CAST-ON: * CO 5 sts, BO 2 sts, slip st rem on right needle back to left needle; rep from *.

Picot Bind-Off

LAST ROW: BO 2 sts, * sl st back to LH needle, using the cable cast-on method, CO 3 sts, then BO 5 sts; rep from *.

Picot Hem **(multiple of 2 stitches + 1)**

Cast on required number of stitches using a provisional cast-on method.

ROWS 1, 3, AND 5: Knit.

ROWS 2, 4, AND 6: Purl.

ROW 7 (TURNING ROW/FOLD LINE): K1, * yo, k2tog; rep from *.

ROWS 8, 10, AND 12: Purl.

ROWS 9, 11, AND 13: Knit.

ROW 14: Unravel provisional cast-on and place free loops on a spare needle, pointing in same direction as last needle worked. Fold and work together 1 st from each needle.

148a–d.

KNITTED PLEATS

General Description:

Pleats are formed by folding knitted fabric back on itself to make three layers and two vertical creases, then knitting the working stitches from each layer of the crease together to make the fold-over permanent. Knitted pleats will not have the same crisp appearance as pressed, sewn pleats in woven fabrics; however, when knit at a fine gauge and blocked vigorously, this method can be used to good effect in knitted projects.

Properties:

This pattern will create a multilayered fabric with reduced drape. Pleats consist of three panels—the front, the turn-back, and the back. The folding edges are created by knitting two slip-stitch columns, which loosens the fabric and makes it more amenable to folding. The stitches between these slipped-stitch columns form the turn-back panel, and the width of the pleat can be changed by increasing or decreasing the number of stitches in the turn-back panel. It is also helpful to know that the (sl 1 wyib) is always used for the front-edge crease, and the (sl 1 wyif) is always used for the back-edge crease.

Yarn Consumption:

This technique can be worked in many stitch patterns and will use the amount of yarn of the stitch pattern chosen. If substituted into a pattern with a flat surface, it will use substantially more yarn, as the width of the pleat is knitted three times to cover a single width.

Suggested Uses:

00–4

Pleats are traditionally found in kilts and other skirts, but consider knitting pleats up the waistband in an empire-waist blouse or small pleats into the edge of fancy gloves.

Pattern: ***Single Pleat L* (panel of 25 stitches)**

WORKING FROM BOTTOM EDGE:

ROW 1 AND ALL OTHER RIGHT-SIDE ROWS: K9, sl 1 wyib, k5, sl 1 wyif, k9.

ROW 2 AND ALL WS ROWS: Purl.

WORK UNTIL PLEATS ARE DESIRED LENGTH, ENDING ON A WRONG-SIDE ROW, THEN CLOSE THE PLEAT:

1. Sl 9 sts to a dpn (these are the front of the pleat).
2. Sl next 6 sts to a 2nd dpn (these are the turn-back stitches).
3. Fold pleat so that fabric is layered from front to back: front stitches, turn-back stitches, back stitches.
4. K3, then work together 1 st from each of the 3 pleat layers until all turn-back stitches are worked.

***Single Pleat R* (panel of 25 stitches)**

WORKING FROM BOTTOM EDGE:

ROW 1 AND ALL OTHER RIGHT-SIDE ROWS: K9, sl 1 wyif, k5, sl 1 wyib, k9.

ROW 2 AND ALL OTHER WRONG-SIDE ROWS: Purl.

WORK UNTIL PLEATS ARE DESIRED LENGTH, ENDING ON A WRONG-SIDE ROW, THEN CLOSE THE PLEAT:

1. Sl 9 sts to a dpn (these are the back of the pleat).
2. Sl next 6 sts to a 2nd dpn (these are the turn-back stitches).
3. Fold pleat so that fabric is layered from front to

back: front stitches, turn-back stitches, back stitches.

4. K3, work together 1 st from each of the 3 pleat layers until all turn-back stitches are worked.

Variation: *Box Pleat* (panel of 44 stitches)
This pattern combines the left and right single pleats to form a double pleat with a square, front-facing panel.

WORKING FROM BOTTOM EDGE:
ROW 1 AND ALL OTHER RIGHT-SIDE ROWS: K9, sl 1 wyif, k5, sl 1 wyib, k12, sl 1 wyib, k5, sl 1 wyif, k9.
ROW 2 AND ALL OTHER WRONG-SIDE ROWS: Purl.
WORK UNTIL PLEATS ARE DESIRED LENGTH, ENDING ON A WRONG-SIDE ROW, THEN CLOSE THE PLEAT:
CLOSE RIGHT PLEAT:

1. Sl 9 sts to a dpn (these are the back of the right pleat).

2. Sl next 6 sts to a 2nd dpn (these are the turn-back stitches).

3. Fold pleat so that fabric is layered from front to back: front stitches, turn-back stitches, back stitches.

4. K3 from back dpn, then work together 1 st from each of the 3 pleat layers until all turned-back stitches are worked.

5. Sl 6 sts to a dpn (these are the front of the left pleat).

6. Sl next 6 sts to a 2nd dpn (these are the turn-back stitches).

7. Fold pleat so that fabric is layered from front to back: front stitches, turn-back stitches, back stitches.

8. Work together 1 st from each of the 3 pleat layers until all turned-back stitches are worked.

Inverted Box Pleat (panel of 44 stitches)
The pleats form a centered vertical slit that hides a square back-facing panel, as if the box pleat was turned back-side front.

WORKING FROM BOTTOM EDGE:
ROW 1 AND ALL OTHER RIGHT-SIDE ROWS: K10, sl 1 wyib, k5, sl 1 wyif, k10, sl 1 wyif, k5, sl 1 wyib, k10.
ROW 2 AND ALL OTHER WRONG-SIDE ROWS: Purl.
WORK UNTIL PLEATS ARE DESIRED LENGTH ENDING ON A WRONG-SIDE ROW, THEN CLOSE THE PLEAT:
Close right pleat:

1. Sl 10 sts to a dpn (these are the front of the right pleat).

2. Sl next 6 sts to a 2nd dpn (these are the turn-back stitches).

3. Fold pleat so that fabric is layered from front to back: front stitches, turn-back stitches, back stitches.

4. K4, then work together 1 st from each of the 3 pleat layers until all turned-back stitches are worked.

5. Sl 6 sts to a dpn (these are the back of the left pleat).

6. Sl next 6 sts to a 2nd dpn (these are the turn-back stitches).

7. Fold pleat so that fabric is layered from front to back: front stitches, turn-back stitches, back stitches.

8. Work together 1 st from each of the 3 pleat layers until all turned-back stitches are worked.

149a–b.

KICK PLEAT

General Description:

Though the standard pleat is infinitely variable, this is an easier way to create a pleated edge, without the complication of folding the fabric and working stitches together.

Properties:

This pattern creates a double-thick fabric, as the decreases fold the fabric back in on itself for an almost ruffled effect. It is essentially a (k4, p3) ribbing with decreases worked in the purl sections every other row until there are no more purl stitches.

Yarn Consumption:

As for a ribbing, the fabric folds back in on itself and requires more yarn than a plain, flat stockinette edge.

Suggested Uses:

00–8

This would be a fun edge to work onto a skirt or perhaps along the edge of a baby's dress. Try changing the frequency of the decreases or the number of stitches in the knit-stitch bands to alter the length and width of the pleats, respectively.

Pattern: **(begin with multiple of 7 stitches + 4; end with multiple of 4 stitches)**

WORKING FROM BOTTOM EDGE:
ROWS 1 AND 3: * K4, p3; rep from *, end k4.
ROWS 2, 4, 6, 8, 10, AND 12: Knit into all knit sts and purl into all purl stitches.
ROW 5: * K4, p2tog, p1; rep from *, end k4.
ROW 7: * K4, p2; rep from *, end k4.
ROW 9: * K4, p2tog; rep from *, end k4.
ROW 11: * K4, p1; rep from *, end k4.
ROW 13: * K3, k2tog; rep from *, end k4.
ROW 14: Purl.

Variation: *Reverse Kick Pleat* (begin with multiple of 7 stitches + 4; end with multiple of 4 stitches)
This is the wrong side of the kick-pleat fabric; its interesting edge has tall, thin, knit-stitch triangles on a bed of reverse stockinette.

WORKING FROM BOTTOM EDGE:
ROWS 1 AND 3 (WS): * K4, p3; rep from *, end k4.
ROWS 2, 4, 6, 8, 10, AND 12: Knit into all knit sts and purl into all purl stitches.
ROW 5: * K4, p2tog, p1; rep from *, end k4.
ROW 7: * K4, p2; rep from *, end k4.

ROW 9: * K4, p2tog; rep from *, end k4.
ROW 11: * K4, p1; rep from *, end k4.
ROW 13: * K3, k2tog; rep from *, end k4.
ROW 14: Purl.

150a–d. 📷 **RUFFLE CAST-ON**

Other Name: Basic k2tog ruffle.

General
Description: This basic ruffle pattern uses one row of decreases to gather the fabric, forcing the rows with a larger amount of stitches to ruffle and protrude from the decrease row.

Properties: This pattern creates a puckered fabric with a flared bottom edge.

Yarn
Consumption: This fabric will use marginally more yarn than stockinette because the decrease row gathers in the fabric.

Suggested Uses: This is yet another pattern conducive to frilly skirt edges and other dainty projects. It is also a particularly useful technique when knitting outfits for a doll clown.

\ 00–8

Pattern: CAST ON double the amount of sts needed.
WORK in stockinette or desired pattern until desired ruffle length, end with a WS row.
NEXT ROW (RS): K2tog across.

Variation:

Ruffle Cast-On Plus or *Basic K3tog Ruffle*
By increasing the number of stitches decreased—take
a second to think about that—this pattern creates a
deeper pucker than the basic k2tog ruffle.

CAST ON 3 times the amount of sts needed.
WORK in stockinette or desired pattern until desired
   length, end with a wrong-side row.
NEXT ROW (RS): K3tog across.

Basic Ruffle Bind-Off
This pattern works down to the bind-off edge and
uses an increase row to create a ruffled effect similar
to the basic ruffle cast-on techniques.

WORK in stockinette or desired pattern until desired
   length to begin ruffle; end with a wrong-side row.
NEXT ROW (RS): * Knit into stitch below next st, then
   knit into next st; rep from *.
WORK in stockinette or desired pattern until desired
   ruffle length.
BIND OFF.

Layered Basic Ruffle
Two strips of basic ruffles are worked and then joined
by working live stitches together to create a ruffled
strip reminiscent of the raging ruffle fashions popular
in the early 1990s.

CAST ON double the amount of sts needed; begin
with a multiple of 4 sts + 1 and end with a multiple of 2 sts + 1.

BOTTOM LAYER:

ROWS 1 (WS) AND 2: Knit.

ROW 3: Purl.

ROW 4: Knit.

Repeat Rows 3 and 4 until piece measures 2^1/$_2$ inches
(6 cm) from beg; end with a wrong-side row.

NEXT ROW (RS): K1, * k3tog, k1; rep from *.

Place sts on a spare needle.

TOP LAYER:

ROWS 1 (WS) AND 2: Knit.

ROW 3: Purl.

ROW 4: Knit.

Repeat Rows 3 and 4 until piece measures 1 inch
from beg; end with a wrong-side row.

NEXT ROW (RS): K1, * k3tog, k1; rep from *.

Place sts on a spare needle.

JOIN LAYERS:

Work together, purling 2 sts together from each of
the two layers until all stitches are joined.

151a–b.

SMALL BELL RUFFLE CAST-ON

General
Description:

Worked from the edge up, this pattern creates a ruffled edge that looks like small bells hanging on strings
against a background of reverse stockinette.

| Properties: | The edge is thick and ruffled, but once the decreases are completed, the fabric is a background of reverse stockinette with thin, vertical lines of knit stitches, giving the fabric definition and structure. |

Yarn Consumption: The deep ruffles curl the fabric into layers, increasing yarn consumption considerably compared with a plain, flat stockinette edge.

Suggested Uses: This cast-on would be particularly pretty as an edging
00–8 on a dress or a skirt. Also try it at the edge of a three-quarter length sleeve for a peasant-blouse effect.

Pattern: **(begin with multiple of 12 stitches + 3; end with multiple of 4 stitches + 3)**

ROW 1: P3, * k9, p3; rep from *.
ROW 2: K3, * p9, k3; rep from *.
ROW 3: P3, * skp, k5, k2tog, p3; rep from *.
ROW 4: K3, * p7, k3; rep from *.
ROW 5: P3, * skp, k3, k2tog, p3; rep from *.
ROW 6: K3, * p5, k3; rep from *.
ROW 7: P3, * skp, k1, k2tog, p3; rep from *.
ROW 8: K3, * p3, k3; rep from *.
ROW 9: P3, * sk2p, p3; rep from *.
ROW 10: K3, * p1, k3; rep from *.
ROW 11: P3, * k1, p3; rep from *.
ROW 12: Repeat Row 10.
Continue in p3, k1 ribbing as desired.

Variation: *Small Bell Ruffle Bind-Off* (multiple of 4 stitches + 3)
Just like the small bell ruffle cast-on but worked from
the top down to the edge of the fabric.

ROW 1: P3, * k1, p3; rep from *.
ROW 2 AND ALL WRONG-SIDE ROWS: Knit all knit sts
    and purl all purl sts.
ROW 3: P3, * inc1, p3; rep from *.
ROW 5: P3, * k1, m1, k1, p3; rep from *.
ROW 7: P3, * k1, m1, k1, m1, k1, p3; rep from *.
ROW 9: P3, * k1, m1, k3, m1, k1, p3; rep from *.
ROW 11: P3, * k1, m1, k5, m1, k1, p3; rep from *.
ROW 12: Repeat Row 2.
Bind off.

152a–b.   **LARGE BELL RUFFLE CAST-ON**

General
Description: Worked up from the edge of the fabric, this pattern
uses decreases within a ribbing base to create a ruffled
border, but to a much different end than kick pleats.
These bold ruffles bulge from the surface of the fabric.

Properties: Large, rounded bell ruffles protrude from a bed of
reverse stockinette. Although the pattern does not
include the knit stitch vertical strips of the small bell
ruffle, they could easily be added if desired.

Yarn
Consumption:

These bulging ruffles push out from the fabric, increasing yarn consumption considerably compared with a plain, flat stockinette edge.

Suggested Uses:

00–10

Though this pattern is another obvious candidate for skirt edges and other dainty applications, try knitting it as the edge of a child's sweater and sewing eyes and little tongues onto each protrusion to create a snake-head edge. Or work the pattern in the round and use as the base of a knitted rocket ship. Experimenting with this decreasing/increasing technique can result in any number of raised objects from a flat surface.

Pattern:

(begin with multiple of 20 stitches + 7; end with multiple of 8 stitches + 7)

ROW 1: P7, * k13, p7; rep from *.
ROW 2: K7, * p13, k7; rep from *.
ROW 3: P7, * skp, k9, k2tog, p7; rep from *.
ROW 4: K7, * p11, k7; rep from *.
ROW 5: P7, * skp, k7, k2tog, p7; rep from *.
ROW 6: K7, * p9, k7; rep from *.
ROW 7: P7, * skp, k5, k2tog, p7; rep from *.
ROW 8: K7, * p7, k7; rep from *.
ROW 9: P7, * skp, k3, k2tog, p7; rep from *.
ROW 10: K7, * p5, k7; rep from *.
ROW 11: P7, * skp, k1, k2tog, p7; rep from *.
ROW 12: K7, * p3, k7; rep from *.
ROW 13: P7, * sk2p, p7; rep from *.

ROW 14: Knit.

Continue in pattern as desired.

Variation: *Large Bell Ruffle Bind-Off* (begin with multiple of 8 stitches + 7)

Just like the large bell ruffle cast-on but worked from the top down to the edge of the fabric.

ROW 1: P7, * kf/b/f, p7; rep from *.
ROW 2: K7, * p2, p1 tbl, k7; rep from *.
ROW 3: P7, * yo, k3, yfrn, p7; rep from *.
ROW 4: K7, * p4, p1 tbl, k7; rep from *.
ROW 5: P7, * yo, k5, yfrn, p7; rep from *.
ROW 6: K7, * p6, p1 tbl, k7; rep from *.
ROW 7: P7, * yo, k7, yfrn, p7; rep from *.
ROW 8: K7, * p8, p1 tbl, k7; rep from *.
ROW 9: P7, * yo, k9, yfrn, p7; rep from *.
ROW 10: K7, * p10, p1 tbl, k7; rep from *.
ROW 11: P7, * yo, k11, yfrn, p7; rep from *.
ROW 12: K7, * p12, p1 tbl, k7; rep from *.
BIND OFF.

153. 📷 **POINT EDGING**

Other Name: Loop edging.

General Description: This lace edging uses yarn-overs and decreases to create a sharply pointed picot lace edging.

Properties: This pattern creates a narrow strip of openwork lace to be sewn or worked onto the edge of a larger lace project. The fabric has excellent drape and little inherent structure.

Yarn Consumption: The strips of yarn-overs draw open the fabric, increasing yarn consumption noticeably.

Suggested Uses: This unassuming pattern would complement any delicate project nicely, making it a suitable edging for not only lace garments but also formal tablecloths, lace table runners, or fancy pillowcases.

Pattern: **CAST ON** 11 sts and knit 1 row.

ROW 1: K3, (yo, ssk, k1) twice, (yo) twice, k1, (yo) twice, k1.

ROW 2: (K2, p1) 4 times, k3. (On this row each double yo is treated as 2 sts, the first being knitted and the second purled.)

ROW 3: K3, yo, ssk, k1, yo, ssk, k7.

ROW 4: BO 4 sts, k3, p1, k2, p1, k3.

---

154. **WAVE LACE EDGING**

General Description: The sibling to print o' the wave, this lace edging forms a series of cresting waves, stylized in the manner seen on prehistoric cave walls and children's drawings.

Properties:	The open fabric has excellent drape and a slightly scalloped bottom edge.
Yarn Consumption:	The strips of yarn-overs draw open the fabric, decreasing yarn consumption considerably.
Suggested Uses:	Pair this pattern with the print o' the wave lace motif to create a sea-themed stole with gorgeous swirling lines. It would also be suitable as a lace edging along the bottom of a lace blouse or sewn along the edge of a pillowcase for the beach house.
Pattern:	**CAST ON** 13 sts.

ROW 1 (WS) AND ALL OTHER WRONG-SIDE ROWS: K2, purl to last 2 sts, k2. (Number of purl sts will vary from row to row.)

ROW 2: Sl 1, k3, yo, k5, yo, k2tog, yo, k2.

ROW 4: Sl 1, k4, sk2p, k2, (yo, k2tog) twice, k1.

ROW 6: Sl 1, k3, ssk, k2, (yo, k2tog) twice, k1.

ROW 8: Sl 1, k2, ssk, k2, (yo, k2tog) twice, k1.

ROW 10: Sl 1, k1, ssk, k2, (yo, k2tog) twice, k1.

ROW 12: K1, ssk, k2, yo, k1, yo, k2tog, yo, k2.

ROW 14: Sl 1, (k3, yo) twice, k2tog, yo, k2.

155.

ZIGZAG LACE EDGING

General Description:	Dating back to the Victorian era, this bold zigzag is four eyelets wide, making it a rather broad edging. It

begins with only 11 stitches but increases to 35 at its zenith.

Properties: The openwork fabric has excellent drape and an uneven left edge.

Yarn Consumption: The wide strips of yarn-overs open up the fabric considerably, decreasing yarn consumption noticeably.

Suggested Uses: The breadth makes this edging more suitable for larger
\ 00–8 lace projects—it might overpower smaller ones. Try also knitting mirror-image panels for a diamond-shaped lace scarf.

Pattern: **CAST ON** 11 sts.
ROW 1: Sl 1 wyif, K2, (yo, k2tog) 3 times, yo, k2.
ROW 2 AND ALL OTHER WRONG-SIDE ROWS: Knit.
ROW 3: Sl 1 wyif, K3, (yo, k2tog) 3 times, yo, k2.
ROW 5: Sl 1 wyif, K4, (yo, k2tog) 3 times, yo, k2.
ROW 7: Sl 1 wyif, K5, (yo, k2tog) 3 times, yo, k2.
ROW 9: Sl 1 wyif, K6, (yo, k2tog) 3 times, yo, k2.
ROW 11: Sl 1 wyif, K7, (yo, k2tog) 3 times, yo, k2.
ROW 13: Sl 1 wyif, K8, (yo, k2tog) 3 times, yo, k2.
ROW 15: Knit.
ROW 17: Sl 1 wyif, K6, (k2tog, yo) 4 times, k2tog, k1.
ROW 19: Sl 1 wyif, K5, (k2tog, yo) 4 times, k2tog, k1.
ROW 21: Sl 1 wyif, K4, (k2tog, yo) 4 times, k2tog, k1.
ROW 23: Sl 1 wyif, K3, (k2tog, yo) 4 times, k2tog, k1.
ROW 25: Sl 1 wyif, K2, (k2tog, yo) 4 times, k2tog, k1.

ROW 27: Sl 1 wyif, K1, (k2tog, yo) 4 times, k2tog, k1.
ROW 29: Sl 1 wyif, (k2tog, yo) 4 times, k2tog, k1.
ROW 30: Knit.

156.

LEAF EDGING

Other Names: Tulip bud edging, scalloped leaves.

General Description: This delightful pattern creates a design resembling leaves growing up and out from the edge of the project. The leaves are the basic lace leaves found in many patterns, but the increases and decreases on the left side mark the edge of the fabric, giving it a scalloped edge.

Properties: This would be best characterized as an eyelet edging, as the majority of the design is formed using the contrast of knit stitches against a background of purl stitches, with eyelets defining the center of each leaf. As a result, the pattern creates a solid, embossed fabric with some structure and a fair amount of drape.

Yarn Consumption: This pattern is essentially a stockinette pattern with spots of reverse stockinette, and it uses approximately the same amount of yarn as stockinette.

Suggested Uses: Try this along the armhole edge of a sleeveless summer blouse to create a unique cap sleeve. It would also be a lovely edge for any leaf-themed lace project.

Pattern: **CAST ON** 8 sts.

ROW 1: K5, yo, k1, yo, k2.

ROW 2: P6, kf/b, k3.

ROW 3: K4, p1, k2, yo, k1, yo, k3.

ROW 4: P8, kf/b, k4.

ROW 5: K4, p2, k3, yo, k1, yo, k4.

ROW 6: P10, kf/b, k5.

ROW 7: K4, p3, k4, yo, k1, yo, k5.

ROW 8: P12, kf/b, k6.

ROW 9: K4, p4, ssk, k7, k2tog, k1.

ROW 10: P10, kf/b, k7.

ROW 11: K4, p5, ssk, k5, k2tog, k1.

ROW 12: P8, kf/b, k2, p1, k5.

ROW 13: K4, p1, k1, p4, ssk, k3, k2tog, k1.

ROW 14: P6, kf/b, k3, p1, k5.

ROW 15: K4, p1, k1, p5, ssk, k1, k2tog, k1.

ROW 16: P4, kf/b, k4, p1, k5.

ROW 17: K4, p1, k1, p6, sk2p, k1.

ROW 18: P2tog, BO 5 sts, p3, k4.

157. 📷 **TWIN LEAF EDGING**

General
Description:

This handsome pattern of layered, paired leaves is designed so that it can be attached to a project from either its left or right edge.

Properties:

This pattern creates a narrow strip of fabric with a surface textured by the shaping of the leaves' edges and the eyelets that form their centers. The shaping also creates a deep scallop along the cast-on edge and a V-shaped point along the bind-off edge.

Yarn Consumption: Because the scattered groups of eyelets do not open the fabric significantly, this pattern uses approximately the same amount of yarn as stockinette.

Suggested Uses: More than twice as wide as the single leaf edging, this pattern would be suitable as an edging for any leaf-themed shawl or stole. Also consider inserting it as a panel into a sweater or blouse.

Pattern: **CAST ON** 22 sts.

ROW 1 (WS) AND ALL SUBSEQUENT WRONG-SIDE ROWS: P10, k2, p10.

ROW 2: K6, k3tog, yo, k1, yo, p2, yo, k1, yo, sk2p, k6.

ROW 4: K4, k3tog, k1, (yo, k1) twice, p2, k1, (yo, k1) twice, sk2p, k4.

ROW 6: K2, k3tog, k12, yo, k1, yo, k2, p2, k2, yo, k1, yo, k2, sk2p, k2.

ROW 8: K3tog, k3, yo, k1, yo, k3, p2, k3, p2, k3, yo, k1, yo, k3, sk2p.

Repeat Rows 1–8 until desired length, bind off.

158. **NARROW VAN DYKE**

General Description: This lace edging has a thin strip of van dyke faggoting separating its sharp, zigzagging border from the main body of the project.

Properties:

This pattern forms a border with sharp, triangular points filled with eyelets. The defined, openwork border has excellent drape.

Yarn
Consumption:

The strip of faggoting combined with the eyelet fill open up the fabric considerably, decreasing yarn consumption substantially.

Suggested Uses:
\ 00–4

This border would offer a nice contrast to lace patterns with less inherent structure, such as snowdrop lace or purse stitch; consider it also as a complement to more geometric lace patterns, such as fern lace or Madeira fans.

Pattern:

CAST ON 7 stitches and knit one row.

ROW 1: Sl 1 wyib, k2, yo, k2tog, (yo) twice, k2tog.

ROW 2: Yo, k2, p1, k2, yo, k2tog, k1.

ROW 3: Sl 1 wyib, k2, yo, k2tog, k4.

ROW 4: K6, yo, k2tog, k1.

ROW 5: Sl 1 wyib, k2, yo, k2tog, [(yo) twice, k2tog] 2 times.

ROW 6: (K2, p1) twice, k2, yo, k2tog, k1.

ROW 7: Sl 1 wyib, k2, yo, k2tog, k6.

ROW 8: K8, yo, k2tog, k1.

ROW 9: Sl 1 wyib, k2, yo, k2tog, [(yo) twice, k2tog] 3 times.

ROW 10: (K2, p1) 3 times, k2, yo, k2tog, k1.

ROW 11: Sl 1 wyib, k2, yo, k2tog, k9.

ROW 12: BO 7, k3, yo, k2tog, k1.
Repeat Rows 1–12 until desired length; bind off.

159. **CYPRESS**

General
Description:

This border pattern is found on the traditional shawls of the British Isles and uses a simple arrangement of eyelets within a bed of garter stitch to create a distinctive design.

Properties:
↔

This pattern forms a raised, textured border; the double yarn-over worked in Row 5 creates small points that jut out from the edges. The vertical and zigzagging strips of eyelets give the fabric considerable lateral stretch.

Yarn
Consumption:

The garter stitch ribbing draws in the fabric, but the effect is more than mitigated by the strips of yarn-overs that open up the fabric; all told, this pattern uses slightly less yarn than stockinette.

Suggested Uses:
\ 00–4

Use this pattern as it was traditionally intended—as a border on a lace shawl or stole—or consider it for a dainty border treatment along the edge of a blouse or pillowcase.

Pattern:
⚠

CAST ON 12 stitches.
ROW 1: Sl 1 wyib, k5, k2tog, yo, k1, k2tog, k1.

ROW 2: K4, yo, k2tog, k2, yo, k2tog, k1.

ROW 3: Sl 1 wyib, k3, k2tog, yo, k1, k2tog, k2.

ROW 4: K7, yo, k2tog, k1.

ROW 5: Sl 1 wyib, k4, yo, k2tog, k1, (yo) twice, k2.

ROW 6: K2, (k1, p1) into double yo of previous row, k2, yo, k3, yo, k2tog, k1.

ROW 7: Sl 1 wyib, k6, yo, k2tog, k4.

ROW 8: BO 2, k2, yo, k5, yo, k2tog, p1.

160. 📷   **ARAN BRAID WITH FRINGE**

Other Name:	Woven braid with fringe.
General Description:	This clever edging is worked much like a regular cable panel, but it has four extra knit stitches added to one side. After the panel has been knit to the desired length and the cable stitches are bound off, the extra stitches are unraveled to create an impressive horizontal fringe.
Properties:	The thick, textured strip of fabric will have a fringe hanging from one of its long sides. It is intended to be knit as a long, vertical strip, which will be turned on its side as a horizontal edging.
Yarn Consumption:	The allover cable pattern draws in the fabric, increasing yarn consumption noticeably.

Suggested Uses:
00–8

Along with sweater and blanket edgings, this stitch would be a neat addition to a knitted bag. Knit a strip twice the width of the desired bag, fold it in half wrong-side facing in, and seam the bottom edge so that the fringe is hanging down. Then pick up stitches along the top edge of the cabled edge and knit in the desired stitch pattern to create the sides of the bag. Handles can be knitted or store bought.

Pattern:

(panel of 12 stitches)

ROWS 1 AND 3 (WS): Purl.
ROW 2: K4, (sl 2 sts to cn and hold in back, k2, then k2 from cn) twice.
ROW 4: K6, sl 2 sts to cn and hold in front, k2, then k2 from cn, k2.
Repeat Rows 1–4 until desired length; end with a RS row. Bind off 7 sts, fasten off 8th st. Sl rem 4 sts off needle and unravel them on every row for fringe. Cut ends of loops and trim as desired.

161a–b.

I-CORD EDGING

General Description:

I-cord is a term coined by knitting genius Elizabeth Zimmerman; the I stands for "idiot," because she called this technique "an idiot's delight" for its simplicity. The cord is created by working a few stitches on a double-pointed needle; at the end of the row, instead of turning the needle around, the stitches are slid to the other end and worked again by bringing the yarn tail around from the far side.

Properties:
The round knitted cord has a smooth stockinette surface. Its length is limited only by the knitter's endurance.

Yarn Consumption:
Plain I-cord is knit in stockinette and uses an equivalent amount of yarn.

Suggested Uses:
\ 00–8
I-cord edging at its simplest can be knit to the length of the project's edge and sewn on plainly. It is often knit in a contrasting color to add interest. For a playful edging, knit the cord longer than the edge of the piece and twist the cord into loops while sewing it on. In this case, the cord will be secured to the project only every inch or so. I-cord can also be used as a drawstring, mitten connectors, or even to top a knitted hat.

Pattern:
CAST ON 5 sts onto a double-pointed needle.
ALL ROWS: K5, at end of row do not turn needle, slide sts to other end of needle.
Knit to desired length. Bind off. Sew or knit onto piece as desired.

Variation:
Eyelet Cord Edging
This pattern creates an I-cord with evenly spaced eyelet holes through which a delicate ribbon can be laced

for added decoration.

CAST ON 5 sts.
ROWS 1, 2, AND 4: K5, at end of row do not turn
  needle, slide sts to other end of needle.
ROW 3: K2, yo, k2tog, k1, at end of row do not turn
  needle, slide sts to other end of needle.

Sources: Books

Eichenseer, Erika, Erika Grill, and Betta Krön. *Omas Strickgeheimnisse*. Munich: Rosenheimer Verlagshaus, 2000.

Epstein, Nicky. *Knitting on the Edge*. New York: Sixth&Spring Books, 2004.

Epstein, Nicky. *Knitting over the Edge*. New York: Sixth&Spring Books, 2005.

Gardiner, Kay, and Ann Shayne. *Mason*Dixon Knitting*. New York: Potter Craft, 2006.

Gibson-Roberts, Priscilla, and Deborah Robson. *Knitting in the Old Way: Designs and Techniques from Ethnic Sweaters*. Boulder, Colorado: Nomad Press, 2004.

Harmony Guides 220 Aran Stitches and Patterns, The. London: Collins & Brown, 1998.

Khmeleva, Galina, and Carol R. Noble. *Gossamer Webs: The History and Techniques of Orenburg Lace Shawls*. Loveland, Colorado: Interweave Press, 1998.

Pearl-McPhee, Stephanie. *Knitting Rules!* North Adams, Massachusetts: Storey Publishing, 2006.

Rutt, Richard. *History of Handknitting*, London: A. B. T. Batsford, 1987.

Sowerby, Jane. *Victorian Lace Today*. Sioux Falls, South Dakota, XRX Books, 2006.

Stanley, Montse. *Reader's Digest Knitter's Handbook: A Comprehensive Guide to the Principles and Techniques of Handknitting*. Pleasantville, New York: Reader's Digest Association, 1993.

Stoller, Debbie. *Stitch 'n' Bitch, The Knitter's Handbook*. New York: Workman Publishing Company, 2003.

Thomas, Mary. *Mary Thomas's Book of Knitting Patterns*. London: Hodder and Stoughton, 1943.

Ultimate Sourcebook of Knitting and Crochet Stitches, The. London: Collins & Brown, 2003.

Vogue Knitting Stitchionary, Volume One: Knit & Purl. New York: Sixth&Spring Books, 2005.

Vogue Knitting Stitchionary, Volume Two: Cables. New York: Sixth&Spring Books, 2006.

Walker, Barbara G. *A Treasury of Knitting Patterns*. New York: Charles Scribner's Sons, 1968.

Walker, Barbara G. *A Second Treasury of Knitting Patterns*. New York: Charles Scribner's Sons, 1970.

Waterman, Martha. *Traditional Knitted Lace Shawls*. Loveland, Colorado: Interweave Press, 1998.

Sources: Web Sites

Industry Leaders

http://www.tkga.com The Knitting Guild Association provides information about upcoming conventions, the Master Knitters Program, and local guilds and clubs.

www.yarnstandards.com Standards and guidelines for knitting and crochet compiled by the Craft Yarn Council of America.

http://www.interweave.com/ Home of Interweave Press, publisher of Interweave Knits magazine. Site includes articles on technique and previews of upcoming issues.

http://www.schoolhousepress.com/ This well-loved publishing house was launched by Elizabeth Zimmerman, the knitting goddess herself. Site includes links to their lengthy catalog of books, as well as information on the famous Knitting Camp.

http://www.vogueknitting.com Site contains basic technique instruction, corrections, and charts associated with the patterns published in this quarterly magazine.

http://www.knitrowan.com Browse and purchase Rowan's high-end yarn and industry-leading pattern books.

http://www.knittygritty.com/ The DIY network's popular knitting show site includes patterns for purchase and instruction on how to apply to appear on the show.

http://www.knitlist.com The original online forum for knitters, this site boasts more than 10,000 members and has existed since 1994.

Who Needs Paper?

www.knitty.com The popular and free online quarterly knitting magazine. Be sure to search the extensive pattern and article archives.

http://www.magknits.com/ Although this free online magazine may not appear as polished as Knitty, pattern gems may still be found in its archives.

http://www.knittersreview.com A free online weekly magazine, featuring yarn reviews, book reviews, polls, patterns, and forums.

How-To

www.knittinghelp.com Free online videos demonstrating basic and advanced knitting techniques.

www.grumperina.com/rightcable.htm Tutorial for cabling without a cable needle with clear, step-by-step photographs. A simple technique that makes knitting a heavily-cabled pattern a much lighter affair.

http://wendyjohnson.net/blog/sockpattern.htm A generic, adjustable toe-up sock pattern. Perfect for when you're not sure how much sock your yarn will make; just knit until the yarn runs out and cast off.

Handy Tools

www.knittingfool.com A virtual smorgasbord of knitting resources, including a pattern generator, stitch pattern catalog, and yarn requirement calculator.

http://www.thedietdiary.com/knittingfiend/KnittersGraph.html Generate proportional knitter's graph paper based on specific gauge measurements.

www.sweaterproject.org/?page_id=602 Helpful tool to generate cable charts from written instructions.

www.jrm.cc/color-palette-generator Upload an image file to generate a color palette.

www.colr.org Excellent site to experiment with colors and color schemes.

http://www.kissyourshadow.com/stripe_maker.php Online engine that produces random stripes based on selected color information.

Shop From Home

www.elann.com Quality yarns at discounted prices.

www.knitpicks.com Affordable, quality store-brand yarns.

www.yarn.com Wide selection of yarns, fiber, and supplies for knitting, spinning, and weaving. Discounts available for bulk purchases.

www.littleknits.com Brand-name yarns, great sale prices.

www.purlsoho.com Online store for a shop in New York City; offers beautiful selection of brand-name yarns.

www.knithappens.com Online store for a shop in Alexandria, Virginia; offers beautiful selection of brand-name yarns.

www.spunkyhats.com High-quality hand-painted and handspun yarns, as well as hand-painted fiber for spinners. Amy works her gifted color sense into small batch production, and you can't go wrong with any of her yarns.

www.helloyarn.com More high-quality hand-painted and handspun yarns, as well as hand-painted fiber for spinners. Adrian's small batch stock goes quickly, particularly her unique, jewel-like sock yarns.

http://www.charmwoven.com Personalized labels for your handknits, including the classic "Handknit by (insert your name here)," with a little picture of yarn and needles.

Know Your Yarn

http://yarndex.com Yarn directory with profiles of more than 3,000 yarns.

www.wiseneedle.com Search the wiseneedle database for consumer yarn reviews.

Knitting for Charity

http://www.afghansforafghans.org Afghans for Afghans provides hand-knit and crocheted blankets, sweaters, hats, mittens, and socks to the beleaguered people of Afghanistan.

http://www.chemocaps.com Seeking to provide soft, hand-knit hats for cancer patients undergoing chemotherapy treatment.

http://www.orphan.org/index.php?id=40 The Orphan Foundation of America's Red Scarf Project sends hand-knit scarves to parentless teens.

http://www.hats4thehomeless.org Hats for the Homeless knits and collects hats, scarves, and gloves throughout the year; these are then distributed to the homeless on the weekend before Christmas at St. Francis Xavier's Soup Kitchen on West 15th Street in New York City.

http://groups.yahoo.com/group/SOCKFORSOLDIERS This group focuses on knitting military-standard black socks for American troops overseas.

http://www.fireprojects.org/dulaan.htm A cooperative effort of Flagstaff International Relief Effort, Mossy Cottage Knits, and the Kunzang Palyul Choling Buddhist community of Sedona to provide the impoverished people of Mongolia with warm, hand-knit blankets and garments.

Other Fun Links

www.thewalkertreasury.wordpress.com A pooling of efforts to illustrate, in color, all five of the Barbara Walker stitch pattern treasuries.

http://www.dailyknitter.com/ Featuring articles, tips, book reviews, a nation-wide calendar of knitting events and daily free patterns, this site has a wide range of knitting resources.

www.ravelry.com While still in beta-testing at the time of this writing, this site is promising to be a powerful online community of knitters, offering the ability to search the community's completed project patterns, view stash inventories, and read linked blog posts.

Index

Numbers in **bold** (for example, **96**) can be used to locate knitting swatches in the photograph section. All other numbers are page numbers.

Acknowledgments

Special thanks to the following for tirelessly knitting the swatches pictured in this book:

Elisa McNamara

Sheila McNamara

Wendy Parisi Roemer

Martha Riegelhaupt

Cassandra Mosle

Maryse Roudier

Melanie Brockert

Debbie Brisson

Kellee Middlebrooks

Johanna Parker

Stephanie Anesi

Claudia Bolgen

Sara Barron-Nichols

Sarah Bible

Maya Mackowiak

Jessica Marshall Forbes

Kate Winslow

Jessica Moynihan

Carole Julius

Beth Sundheim

mamacate

Donna Pawlowski

Kristen Mitchell

Kris Liberman

That Laurie Osborne

Kristen Welsh

Their dedication, patience, friendship, and humor make this volume an impressive example of many hands turning an impossible task into light work.

Additional thanks to

Elann.com for generously supplying their Peruvian Highland Wool and Peruvian Highland Silk for use in the swatches

Kevin Kosbab, for never making me feel like an inexperienced first-time author (even though I was an inexperienced first-time author) and for always appreciating the quirks of knitting

Karen Onorato, for her clever and inspired design work and photography

My father, Jeff Cunningham, for his unhesitating encouragement and support

My mother, Kathy Cunningham, for her example of hard work and discipline, making anything possible

And to my husband, Eric, for his unwavering love, patience, and support despite the invasion of countless knitting books, mountains of swatching yarn, and armies of knitters, and for keeping the kitchen clean despite it all

Table of Equivalencies

NEEDLE SIZES

U.S.	Metric	UK
00	1.75	15
0	2	14
1	2.25	13
2	2.75	12
-	3	11
3	3.25	10
4	3.5	-
5	3.75	9
6	4	8
7	4.5	7
8	5	6
9	5.5	5
10	6	4
10.5	6.5	3
-	7	2
-	7.5	1
11	8	0
13	9	00
15	10	000

LENGTH

Inches	Centimeters
1/4	0.65
1/2	1.25
1	2.50
2	5.00
3	7.50
4	10.0
5	12.5
6	15.0
7	17.5
8	20.5
9	23.0
10	25.5
12	30.5
15	38.0

More Quirk Field Guides

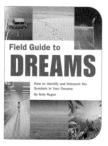

Available Wherever Books Are Sold